# The Music Merchants

# THE
# MUSIC
# MERCHANTS

*Milton Goldin*

The Macmillan Company
Collier-Macmillan Ltd., London

Library of Congress Catalog Card Number: 75-80302

First Printing

The Macmillan Company
Collier-Macmillan Canada Ltd., Toronto, Ontario

Printed in the United States of America

TO *Aranka, Karen* AND *David*

# Contents

## PART THREE: ORGANIZERS

### VII.  *WHOLESALERS AND RETAILERS*

### VIII.  *SPEND SOME*

### EPILOGUE: THE PERFORMING ARTS
### IN A GREAT SOCIETY

# *Preface*

THIS BOOK IS about the business of music in America. The objective is to examine informally the history of opera houses, orchestras, impresarios and patrons, and to come to some conclusions about the way musical institutions have been molded. Admittedly much more could be said on nearly every subject covered. Maurice Grau, Arthur Judson, the New York Academy of Music, each and many other impresarios, opera houses and concert halls deserve entire chapters, books, even sets of volumes.

If I go back twenty-five years to a time when I played the violin in symphony orchestras, I have literally dozens of musicians to thank for anecdotes about artists, opinions of conductors and anguished complaints about impresarios. More recently, I would like to thank the following individuals, who generously gave me their time and searched their memories: Kenneth Allen, Herbert Barrett, Martin Bernstein, Benjamin Boretz, Carl Dahlgren, Hy Faine, Muriel Francis, Joseph Fuchs, Mrs. Virginia Gorodnitzky, Jay Harrison, Israel Horowitz, William M. Judd, Arthur Judson, Jan La Rue, Ruth O'Neill, Harold L. Oram, J. Warren Tapscott, Thomas W. Thompson, Richard Yarnall and Laurence Wasserman.

I also offer special thanks to my father, Hyman Goldin, a musician who early inculcated a belief in me that a symphony orchestra is an almost sacred institution. Above all, thanks are given to my wife, Aranka, whose persistence in seeking (often, insisting on) clarification of details is one of the main reasons for whatever merit the work has.

MILTON GOLDIN

# The Music Merchants

# Prologue: An Early Desideratum

"In truth, were all America like this fair city [New York], and all, no, only a small proportion of its population like the friends we left there, I should say, that the land was the fairest in the world."

—MRS. FRANCES TROLLOPE,
The Domestic Manners of the Americans, *1831*

## 1. *What, therefore, was my delight*

NEW YORK WAS the largest city in the United States in 1825, the year the Erie Canal opened ushering in a great period of commercial development. Governor De Witt Clinton was roundly attacked by political opponents for spending over $7 million on the waterway, but the Erie would repay its cost to taxpayers within a decade. Instead of three weeks, it was to take only eight days to go from New York to Buffalo. New York became the Eastern terminus of the fastest route to Midwestern produce, markets and homesteads. "A cent and a half a mile, a mile and a half an hour" was the way Manhattan's merchants and travelers described the cost and speed of a trip on the waterway.

As in no other American city, commerce and trade set the tone of life in New York. It was where the "trading classes" made fortunes and where real estate speculation was a way of life. A Scottish printer, who had lived in New York, wrote that a person had to be "wide awake" not to break his legs "by running foul of the numberless moveable and immoveable incumbrances" on the sidewalks of the city. A young lady told a Royal Navy officer that "Commission Merchants" were the best marriage prospects. Merchants displaced landed aristocrats as social leaders, and a French economist emphasized the importance of "the industry, the capital, the intelligence, and the enterprise of that, numerically speaking, insignificant minority of Wall Street and Pearl Street."

The metropolis also had its rustic aspects. Fourteenth Street was its northern boundary; above that, Manhattan was farms, orchards and cornfields. Dogs and pigs roamed the streets at will, and thoroughfares were dirty, cluttered and smelly. At City Hall, justice smoked a "segar," much as he would in any county seat on the frontier; an English visitor at a trial was "stupefied with smoke."

Visitors made the same complaints about New York as have been heard during the rest of its history. Its storekeepers were indifferent, its inhabitants were rowdy and vulgar, and its cost of living was too high. Natives offered counter-arguments that became standard: New York was a fine place to live and strangers came at least partly for cultural reasons. "New York [is] the Paris of America," one guidebook writer boasted. "Like that gay and splendid emporium of fashion and literature, New York is constantly filled with strangers, who are drawn hither by the celebrity of our institutions, our commerce, opulence, and multiplied sources of rational pleasure."

Such smug self-esteem was thought justified by the city's upper circles. New York had far outstripped Boston and Philadelphia, its nearest rivals, in wealth and population and was setting fashions for the entire country in architecture, literature and the arts. It was a creative, cosmopolitan city, with an "electric thrill" in the air.

Elsewhere in the nation—notably Boston and Philadelphia— there was nonetheless a persistent belief that New Yorkers had little real aptitude for intellectual and cultural pursuits. John Adams, second President of the United States, and a fussy, hot-tempered Bostonian, thought that "with all the opulence and splendor of this city, there is very little good breeding to be found." As early as 1774, Adams found Gothamites speaking "very loud, very fast, and altogether." If a New Yorker asked a question he never gave the recipient a chance to reply before he again began talking.

Nobody sympathized more with this lack of appreciation for the finer things New York had to offer than Lorenzo Da Ponte, a talkative seventy-six-year-old Jewish-Italian immigrant, who had been court poet to the Emperor of Austria, confidant of Casanova and author of Mozart's libretti for *Don Giovanni, Cosi fan Tutte* and *Le Nozze di Figaro*. Courtly, handsome, well-built and toothless, Da Ponte had passed through the Philadelphia Custom House in early June, 1805, after a fifty-seven day trip from London which was "long, disastrous and full of annoyances and strain."

One annoyance was the steady loss of six dollars a day playing games of chance with a fellow traveler, a merchant from Philadelphia. Da Ponte debarked armed only with a box of violin strings, a set of Italian classics, some other books and about fifty dollars in cash.

The episode was typical of the poet, a speculator handicapped by an artistic temperament, an artist handicapped by a gambler's need to test his luck. In Venice, Vienna, Brussels and London, Da Ponte had regularly smarted from disastrous financial losses in cultural and business undertakings, usually after the most promising beginnings. He was an inveterate gossip forced to endure gossipy associates. He had departed the British capital hounded by creditors after the failure of a bookstore and the circulation of an anonymous letter accusing him of twelve crimes, including murder.

Da Ponte settled in Elizabeth, New Jersey, in Philadelphia and in Sunbury, Pennsylvania, where he invested in several enterprises including a grocery store, a millinery shop, and a distillery. He also lived in New York, where he taught Latin, Italian and Greek. He was only temporarily successful at commerce and was constantly involved in litigations. In 1818, Da

Ponte returned to Philadelphia with the intention "to spread the language and literature of my country . . . ," but in 1819, he disgustedly quit Philadelphia for good. The poet traveled across New Jersey to the banks of the Hudson "with empty purse, but with a heart overflowing with hope and joy . . . [and] saluted from the opposite bank of its beautiful stream, the noble, populous, and to me beloved, city of New York."

Da Ponte was no stranger to Gotham. In 1807 the Da Pontes had been the hit of the New York social season, thanks equally to the poet's droll ways and to his wife's exceptional Italian cuisine. Sophisticated, impeccably groomed European gentlemen were rarities on the local scene, as were Italian cooks.

Da Ponte, who could talk endlessly of his experiences, must have seemed a miracle to wealthy but provincial New Yorkers who made up the city's social elite—Verplancks, Livingstons, Cottenets, Onderdoncks. He had met emperors, dukes, countesses and opera singers. Here was a man who had not only heard a grand opera but had actually written words for grand operas by Mozart. Da Ponte was appointed Professor of Italian Literature at Columbia, taught Italian to the best families, began publishing his *Memoirs* and delivered an oration before "one of the most numerous assemblages of wit and fashion which ever graced an apartment in this city." Yet he was dissatisfied.

"Though, to my joy, I could see the interest in Italian letters increasing daily both in New York and other cities of the Union, I still thought there was another way of making them both more widely spread and more highly esteemed; but, to tell the truth, I did not dare to hope for such a thing," he wrote. "What, therefore, was my delight [in 1825] when a number of persons assured me that the famous Garzia [sic], with his incomparable daughter [Maria Malibran] and several other Italian singers, was coming from London to America, and in fact to New York, to establish Italian opera there—the *desideratum* of my greatest zeal?"

Da Ponte had talked about grand opera with all his society friends. One avid listener was Dominick Lynch, a wealthy wine importer, who then went to London to engage an operatic troupe to appear in New York. He offered García sums that were "past belief." The London *Harmonicon* prophesied that "We have hitherto been the laughing stocks of Europe, for the preposterous manner in which we pay foreign singers, but the ridicule will now be transferred to the Western continent."

Lynch and other very cultured New Yorkers had enjoyed drama of a high order since Colonial times—England's most distinguished actors and actresses appeared regularly—but musically they were less well off. Ballad opera, introduced locally in 1750, was still the mainstay of musical theater. Travelers from Europe brought back stories about the new rage, grand opera, but up to 1825 no local impresario had stepped forward to produce one. John Jacob Astor is said to have attempted to bring Rossini to America in a moment of enthusiasm, but the only hints of future delights were adaptations in English of such masterpieces as Rossini's *Il Barbiere di Siviglia*, Mozart's *Le Nozze di Figaro* and Weber's *Der Freischütz*. These were given abbreviated presentations peppered with popular songs of the day, and followed by comic afterpieces.

Moreover, Manuel del Popolo Vincente García was one of the great tenors of the time, an artist welcome at the leading opera houses of England, France, Italy and Spain. Rossini himself had created several roles for him, including Almaviva in *Il Barbiere*. Everywhere García dominated productions, infusing conductors, casts, choruses and orchestras alike with his own driving enthusiasm.

García, in turn, was bringing with him his daughter, Maria, better known to posterity by her married name, Maria Malibran. The girl was only seventeen, and at the dawn of her career in 1825, but she could already cope with the most difficult roles in the repertory. Her voice was not her only asset; it was claimed that her figure could be studied for "an improvement" on the Venus de Milo.

García's own reasons for bringing troupe and daughter to

New York are unclear. The city was hardly a stop on the international musical circuit. London appearances had not been especially successful, however. At fifty, he may have lost some of his vocal powers and thought success inevitable only before unsophisticated Americans. What probably motivated him most was the guarantee that Lynch and Stephen Price, manager of the Park Theatre, were willing to pay.

## 2. *Everything pleased*

The Park Theatre, where García's troupe would make its debut on November 29, 1825, was New York's leading house and the second theater with the same name located uptown at 21-15 Park Row, near Ann Street. The first Park nobly served drama from 1798 until 1820, when it was destroyed by fire. The new Park, opened in 1821, was already well on its way to theatrical fame. The year before García arrived it featured a melodrama in which the leading lady rode a horse across a chasm, the earliest "horse opera" on record.

Customers considered the Park's lyre-shaped interior and three chandeliers "magnificent" and patronized its second-floor saloon, but they were noisy and boisterous, reflecting frontier ways. Carefree theatergoers, mostly men, sometimes spat on the floor but always kept their hats on their heads to prevent thefts by light-fingered enthusiasts. The house reeked of tobacco, and it was not unusual for audiences to indicate dissatisfaction with a performance by pelting artists with stones, vegetables and other objects.

Neither the Park nor any other New York theater had ever been host to so glamorous a troupe as García's, and customers were to be on their best behavior at his presentations. Other local theatrical customs were also changed. No comic after-pieces were offered operagoers. The starting time for the performance was set at the late hour of 8 P.M. Playgoers had paid fifty cents per ticket; operagoers paid the "prohibitive" price of $2.00 for a box seat.

Thanks partly to high prices (García was to earn about $3,000), it was an audience of the moneyed and fashionable that arrived at the Park on opening night to hear Rossini's *Il Barbiere*, the first Italian opera sung in the original language in an authentic style in the city. "An assemblage of ladies so fashionable, so numerous and so elegantly dressed [has] probably never been witnessed in an American theater," wrote one of the city's earliest opera critics. Joseph Bonaparte, ex-king of Spain, then living in New Jersey, and James Fenimore Cooper, America's leading writer, were also on hand to hear García as Almaviva, his daughter Maria as Rosina, his son Manuel, Jr., as Figaro, and his wife as Berta.

Both upper-class America and the press were staggered by the experience. Anyone who talked during the music was castigated by his neighbors. "In what language shall we speak of an entertainment so novel in this country?" asked a reporter. "Until it is seen, it will never be believed that a play can be conducted in *recitative* or singing and yet appear nearly as natural as the ordinary drama. We were last night surprised, delighted, enchanted, and such were the feelings of all who witnessed the performance."

It was noted that the orchestra was not always in tune or in time, but an unheard-of number of select musicians—twenty-four—made up the band. García had worked hard for a month drilling them.

The singers made the greatest impression. Audiences were astounded by García's "masterly powers," by the "expressive, characteristic and unceasing gesticulation" of other male members of the troupe, by the "chasteness and propriety" of female performers. Above all, Maria Malibran was a "magnet that attracted all eyes and won all hearts. She seems to use a 'cunning pattern of excelling nature,' equally surprising [audiences] by the melody and tones of her voice and by the propriety and grace of her acting."

During the following months, twice weekly García presented *Il Barbiere*, works by himself, and then Rossini's *Otello, Tancredi* and *La Cenerentola*, at the Park and then at the

Bowery Theatre. Details of production were handled by members of the troupe. The scenery for *Tancredi,* painted by a singer, was acclaimed "of matchless vigor and beauty, displaying magnificent ruins, paintings, etc., so peculiar to modern Italy." García's portrayal of Otello was so convincing at one performance that Maria, who took the role of Desdemona, whispered to him in Spanish, "For God's sake, father, don't kill me." Edmund Kean, the celebrated actor, came backstage after the first performance of the opera, complimented the cast and then invited it to attend *his* appearance in Shakespeare's *Othello* the following night.

Da Ponte called on García and announced himself Mozart's librettist. He promptly heard a rendition of "Finch' han del vino" from *Don Giovanni.* After the artistic treat, Da Ponte suggested that García present *Don Giovanni* in its entirety. "If we have enough actors to give *Don Giovanni,* let us give it soon. It's the best opera in the world!" cried García. Da Ponte, likewise pleased, cried out with joy though partly "from a keen desire, natural enough in me, to see some drama of mine presented on the stage in America."

The company lacked a tenor for the role of Ottavio. Da Ponte, his pupils and his friends raised money to hire one. In his typical erratic fashion García, a tenor, assayed the role of Don Giovanni, a baritone. His son, a baritone, was assigned the role of Leporello, a bass. Maria was cast as Zerlina. The performance on May 23, 1826, was accounted a success though the hired tenor was a miserable failure, and the presentation fell apart at the end of the first act as soloists, orchestra and chorus took different roads. Sword in hand, García threatened the conductor and the finale was repeated. "Everything pleased, everything was admired and praised . . . ," says Da Ponte. The poet translated the libretto into English and sold a "prodigious number" of copies.

García returned to Rossini operas and to some creations of his own on Tuesday and Saturday evenings. Over a ten-month period he was to give seventy-nine performances in all, including forty of the fantastically successful *Il Barbiere*. The troupe's earnings per evening ranged from $250 to $1,962; total receipts were $56,685. There was some talk that it might even settle permanently in New York, but on September 30 the season finally ended with a particularly fine *Barbiere*. In early October García and his troupe left for Mexico.

The troupe, that is, with the exception of Maria, who had married a French merchant named François Eugène Malibran, aged fifty. Manuel García was opposed to the match, not because the prospective groom was thirty years older than his daughter but because he would be deprived of her earnings. Malibran offered García a gift of 100,000 francs, was wed to Maria, and went bankrupt. The girl decided to remain and to pay off her husband's debts. Wild with rage, García abandoned her.

Maria was a hardy type. She renewed her study of English and took to the stage of the Bowery Theatre in English ballad opera. She also joined a choir, and for nearly a year, until she returned to Europe, the most fascinating, voluptuous, enchanting prima donna of the first half of the nineteenth century sang hymns at New York's Grace Church.

### 3. *A style of magnificence*

García's success thrilled Da Ponte, a knight errant in the service of culture. Nonetheless the poet was pained by the cultural apathy of New York's multitudes. "What marvel," he says in his *Memoirs*, "that certain arias of Vaccai, Generali, and of others of their order, beautiful as they were, were not generally admired in America. . . ." A people accustomed "previously to hearing only the songs and ballads of Kelly, or Polish, Scottish, or Irish airs, with, of course, the most favorite national anthem, 'Yankee Doodle,'" could hardly understand the works of masters. Da Ponte received "propositions" from impresarios in Italy to mount productions in New York.

He discouraged interest "forseeing that they would not be compatible with the character and customs of this city." Instead the poet replied with propositions of his own.

Da Ponte was not simply trying to discourage competition. Interest in Italian opera fell off sharply after García left New York. The fashionable world was "surprised, delighted, enchanted"; but "adapted," abbreviated versions in English of recent hits such as *Don Giovanni, Il Barbiere* and *La Cenerentola* came back into style. In 1828, a visiting German musician found that "the performance of a whole opera is not to be thought of"; the *New York Gazette and Phi Beta Kappa Repository* had long since dismissed Italian opera as "a forced and unnatural bantling" unsuited to American tastes.

A major question for the *Gazette,* social leaders, and the multitudes alike was why they should attend opera sung in Italian, a language few understood. Everybody could understand a shapely prima donna no matter what her language, but voluptuous artists who sang in Italian, like Malibran, were in short supply. There seemed no good reason to substitute opera in Italian for opera in English.

Meanwhile, New York's theater orchestras, well stocked with brass instruments, continued to rely heavily on Italian repertory, however. "The great *Maestro* himself [Rossini], passionately fond as he is of [the trombone] would have shrunk from the overwhelming crash that deafened the ears of the astonished natives." Thus a correspondent for the English periodical *Harmonicon* wrote home after a noisy performance in 1828.

Da Ponte was hard put to think up a solution to this puzzler of language too, but such problems do not deter knight errants, and in 1832, busy with a bookstore, he induced a French tenor named Jacques Montrésor to produce a season of Rossini operas at the Richmond Hill Theatre, a mansion once owned by Aaron Burr. The season, which included the debut of Edelaide Pedrotti, a winsome soprano, and the premiere of Rossini's *L'Italiana in Algieri,* lasted only thirty-five performances. "For the worn and dirty finery at the Park, we had new and appropriate dresses," wrote one reporter, but public response was weak. Da Ponte and Montrésor repaired to Philadelphia's Chestnut Street Theatre to present Italian opera there.

The failure discouraged Montrésor, but not Da Ponte, from further efforts to realize a prime *desideratum,* the establishment of Italian opera. In 1833, at the age of eighty-four, the poet raised $150,000 for the Italian Opera House at the corner of Church and Leonard streets, New York's first theater intended solely for opera. A partner, Chevalier Rivafinoli, was also acquired to recruit singers and musicians.

At once there was a departure from the best European practices. Not only was the house located in one of the city's worst neighborhoods, but unlike continental houses, it was to enjoy no municipal subventions or subsidies from aristocrats anxious to impress guests with the pomp and glamour of their establishments. Permanent opera was introduced to New York on a strictly commercial basis, an attitude in keeping with the business center of the nation. Sponsors made contributions to build the house. Then they received exclusive use of boxes and free tickets for all performances. Impresarios covered production and house costs and leased the premises.

For his core group of sixteen sponsors, who advanced $6,000 each, Da Ponte provided a house of European luxury consistent with grand institutions in Venice, Rome and London. The sponsors held a drawing for boxes. Philip Hone, sometime mayor of New York and winner of one third of Box Number 8, confided to his diary that "The house is superb, and the decorations of the proprietors' boxes (which occupy the whole of the second tier) are in a style of magnificence which even the extravagance of Europe has not equalled." Hundreds of "commodious" sofas and orchestra seats were covered with blue damask. Representations of muses were painted on the dome, and "the scenery and curtains were beautiful beyond precedent."

Outside, the house was less impressive. "The exterior," said Hone, "has nothing to boast of. It is a large brick edifice, very plain and unpretending, and the subscribers' money has not been spent to please the eyes of non-subscribers."

The Italian Opera House was opened on November 18, 1833, with Rossini's *La Gazza Ladra*. New York's richest and most fashionable music lovers attended but immediately doubted whether opera was the right tenant. "To me," Hone wrote in his diary, "it was tiresome and the audience was not excited to any violent degree of applause. The performance occupied four hours—much too long, according to my notion, to listen to a language which one does not understand." Hone asked gloomily, "Will this splendid and refined amusement be supported in New York? I am doubtful."

Another doubtful writer wondered in print if "perhaps an unfortunate circumstance of the success of Italian Opera in this city is, that, at its first introduction, it broke upon us at once in nearly all its perfection. The first company contained some of the finest singers that Europe produced, artists who had secured the applause of the most fashionable audiences of Europe."

Da Ponte and Rivafinoli advertised forty performances at the Italian Opera House with a supplementary post-series offering of twenty-eight performances that brought the season to July 21, 1834. Works by Rossini, Pacini and Cimarosa, conducted by a musician named Salvioni, were offered at admission prices from fifty cents to two dollars. Fifteen performances were also scheduled in Philadelphia. The enterprise was acclaimed a cultural high point in local history in both cities.

Socially and artistically successful, Da Ponte and Rivafinoli were driven from management at the end of only one season. Production costs had totaled $81,054.98; receipts were only $51,780.89. Over $15,000 in ticket receipts was lost in free tickets to the contributors, and losses were borne by the impresarios. It was announced that the house would be let to

Signor Sacchi and Signor Porto, erstwhile Rivafinoli employees, the following season.

In a statement to the press, Rivafinoli set forth his costs, proving conclusively that strictly commercial opera was unfeasible, at least for promoters. Da Ponte set forth his miseries in a letter, proving that he was surrounded by wretches with no appreciation of culture.

"I cannot now remain in silence while my fellow countrymen are sacrificed, the citizens of two noble cities deceived, and an enterprise for which I have so long and ardently labored, so calculated to shed luster on the nation, and so honorable in its commencement, [is] ruined by those who have no means, nor knowledge, nor experience," he cried. Rivafinoli was denounced as an "imprudently daring adventurer"; Porto and Sacchi were plainly bumpkins. "For God's sake let the past become a beacon light to save you from the perils of the future," counseled the poet. "Do not destroy the most splendid ornament of your city."

The second season at the Italian Opera House had just begun when Hone again took to his diary. "The opera [*La Straniera* by Bellini] did not please me. There was too much reiteration, and I shall never discipline my taste to like common colloquial expressions of life: 'How do you do, madame?' or 'Pretty well, I thank you, sir,' the better for being given with orchestral accompaniment." Hone decided that all the box holders could get for their $6000 investments was a "sort of aristocratical distinction." This was hardly enough to justify support.

Just as financial disaster loomed a second time at the Italian Opera House the prima donna, Clementina Fanti, suddenly quit New York. Porto and Sacchi canceled the season and the house became a legitimate theater. In 1836 it was renamed the National Theatre and reopened as home base for James Wallack, a prominent actor-manager. The National, which "exceeded in scenery and costume," burned down in 1839. It was not rebuilt. Its creator, Da Ponte, died the year before, still a teacher of Italian at Columbia.

## 4. *Everybody could see*

"Never again will New York be without this type of artistic pleasure," said one newspaper after García's debut, but following two unsuccessful attempts to establish a permanent company that would sing Italian opera in Italian, New York's impresarios remained content to produce Italian operas sung in English. For ten years, no further attempts were made. Then, in 1844, Ferdinand Palmo, a restaurateur, remodeled Stoppani's Arcade Baths on Chambers Street into an 800-seat "bijou of a theatre" with two private boxes, renamed the structure Palmo's Opera House, and offered up the first performance of *I Puritani*.

The Chambers Street district was infested with gangs of hoodlums, and Palmo arranged for patrons to have coach service with police protection as far north as Forty-Second Street. Despite this service, and some of the best singers New York had yet heard, Palmo was forced to close his opera house during its second season. "Thirty-two professors" in the orchestra had gone on strike for their unpaid wages in one of the city's earliest musicians' strikes. Palmo's property was attached.

It was at Palmo's (under new management) that the first of Verdi's operas to be heard in New York was given. *I Lombardi* competed with Phineas T. Barnum's Mexican War exhibit of Santa Ana's wooden leg, "taken by the American Army and brought to the City by a Gentleman direct from the city of Veracruz." Barnum got more customers than Verdi, but *I Lombardi* ran nine straight performances, no mean record. The *New York Evening Post* thought it likely that from "its showy character" it might even become a local favorite, but the *Albion* dissented: "[Verdi], like all modern Italian writers, is a victim to a passion for instruments of brass and percussion."

Scarcely had *I Lombardi* completed its run when a new

troupe, the Havana Opera Company, arrived from Cuba under the management of Don Francisco Marty y Torrens, an ex-pirate, ex-fishing-fleet tycoon, ex-slave trader, ex-financier and ex-government benefactor. Marty, who received a guarantee from William Niblo, another restaurateur interested in music, presented his troupe at the Park Theatre, now a decrepit building unsuited "for the assemblage of elegant people for elegant pleasure." Its boxes were compared to "pens for beasts." Yet large audiences attended Marty's presentations of *Norma*, *La Sonnambula*, *Mosè in Egitto* and *Ernani*, the first Verdi opera to become popular in New York and one for which Society immediately developed a special affection.

Marty's success was due to a splendid troupe, possibly the finest yet to appear in the New World. It included Fortunata Tedesco, a soprano whose "splendid bust and exquisitely molded arms" dazzled the gentleman from the *Albion*. Luigi Arditi, composer of the ever-popular *Il Bacio*, was the conductor. Cuban impresario and troupe gave considerable impetus to local opera; thanks to their success and to *Ernani's* popularity, another attempt for a permanent opera company was to be made.

The Astor Place Opera was sponsored by one hundred and fifty citizens of "social prominence," who banded together and pledged to support seventy-five evenings of opera each year for five years. Among them was John Jacob Astor, the richest man in America. The terms of support were similar to those at the Italian Opera House. Again, impresarios covered all production and house costs.

The Astor Place Opera was located uptown at Astor Place and Eighth Street, testifying to the relentless northward thrust of the populace. It was an architectural example of the neo-Greek rage that swept New York during the 1830s and 1840s, when Americans began to equate their country with ancient Greece. Jacksonian democrats found parallels between themselves and Athenians of the Golden Age. Grecian styles became the cornerstone of cultivated taste.

The house had 1,800 seats, good acoustics and excellent ventilation. But its prime feature was its glamour, a quality not known to be emphasized at the finest ancient theaters. "Everybody could see, and, what is of infinitely greater consequence, could be seen," wrote Max Maretzek, its conductor and sometime impresario from 1847 to 1850. "Never, perhaps, was any theatre built that afforded a better opportunity for a display of dress." Admittance was restricted to the *haute monde*, who wore kid gloves; lesser citizens dubbed it the "kid glove opera house."

The Astor Place opened with *Ernani* on November 22, 1847, to an audience "generally diffused [with an] air of good breeding," earlier instructed that "carriages will set down with the horses' heads from Broadway and take up in the reverse order." Despite such careful planning its initial impresarios, Messrs. Sanquirico and Patti, barely completed the 1847–48 season before going bankrupt. The following season, Edward Fry, a bookkeeper, took the helm. He promptly went bankrupt too, continuing a local operatic tradition.

William Niblo, owner of Niblo's Garden, an emporium at Broadway and Prince streets where audiences enjoyed cherry cobblers during musical presentations, took the lease in 1848. Niblo presented Donetti's trained-dog act and was served with an injunction by enraged owners on grounds that he violated provisions of the lease. At the hearing Donetti testified that his dogs had appeared before kings and princes. Witnesses declared under oath that the animals were better behaved than many artists. Even Maretzek agreed.

The injunction was dismissed to howls of laughter in the press. In May 1849 the Astor Place, symbol of privilege, was the scene of riots when gangs of toughs battled militia to protest appearances by an English actor, William Charles Macready, thought to have made anti-American remarks. Now the house was a joke in a neighborhood considered unsafe.

When the Astor Place Opera closed its doors in 1850, after

only three seasons, there was a general belief among opera-goers that neither Donetti nor the riots were to blame, however. Don Francisco Marty y Torrens had returned to town from Cuba, bringing with him another fine operatic troupe. "At last we have the grand Italian opera in New York and no, no, no mistake," cried the *Herald*. "They came not to make money but to make mischief," complained Maretzek, well aware of the formidable competition.

Marty's company appeared first at Niblo's Garden and then at Castle Garden, a circular fort off the tip of Manhattan that had been converted to a theater and summer garden earlier the same year. From July until September the Havana company made good use of the theater's 5,000-seat capacity (10,000 people could be accommodated sitting and standing), offering up opera at prices as low as fifty cents per ticket. Patrons ate ice cream and watched fireworks and balloon ascensions as well as opera performances. Even Hone, a snob who disdained contact with the masses, confessed in his diary that Castle Garden was "the most splendid and the largest theatre" he ever saw.

The success inspired Maretzek to hire most of Marty's principal singers and to present them at Castle Garden himself. In three months Maretzek managed to lose $22,000. Undaunted, he continued to be active in bringing music to the masses. Maretzek "the Magnificent," as he came to be known locally, was to be the first impresario in America to conduct his own presentations. He was also to introduce many European artists to American audiences, at prices from fifty cents to two dollars per ticket.

## 5. *A Good Thing*

Though much fumbling and misunderstanding characterized the first quarter-century of grand opera in New York, there were great advances in this as in other musical areas.

In 1850 operagoers crowded Castle Garden for Marty's company, eager to hear his artists. Elsewhere in the city, choral societies gave programs of Handel and Mendelssohn oratorios, and in 1842, a Connecticut Yankee with the euphonious name Ureli Corelli Hill had joined some German immigrants to help found the New York Philharmonic, eventually to become the oldest symphony orchestra in the world.

But if progress was made in developing the institutions of musical life in the nation's wealthiest city, leadership in equal quantity was not displayed in providing them with secure economic bases. Even accepting the inevitable failures of initial efforts, there was a particularly stubborn inability on the part of the social elite to think of musical organizations in any way but a strictly commercial one. New York's aristocrats of the 1830s and 1840s invested in an opera house with the same spirit they invested in any business enterprise, a major objective being returns in the form of free tickets. Again and again strict business principles were proclaimed and applied, only to prove totally useless. As much as possible, losses were afterwards passed on to impresarios, who were least able to meet them.

Music being regarded vaguely as a Good Thing, there was honest confusion whether it should be considered a Good Thing as a business, as a popular entertainment like a circus or as an affectation of the rich. Out of the tangle there would emerge a musical life in which elements of all three approaches were fused, leading to further contradictions and confusion.

It was no accident that P. T. Barnum, America's greatest showman, devised and established the promotional devices that would be used in American musical life for decades.

# PART ONE
## *Impresarios*

# I. *The Zenith of Her Life*
# *and Celebrity*

*"How were the circus receipts today at Madison Square Garden?"*
—P. T. BARNUM'S *last words*

## 1. *They won't believe it at first*

IN OCTOBER 1849, P. T. Barnum, who was dazzling customers with freaks and hoaxes at his American Museum on Broadway at Ann Street in New York, suddenly decided to entice Jenny Lind, the "Swedish Nightingale," to tour the United States under his management. Barnum had never met the soprano and was yet to hear her sing. He heard about her in 1844, 1845 and 1846, while touring England and France with his celebrated midget, General Tom Thumb. Because he was always interested in star performers, Barnum followed Lind's career with interest, noting particularly the furor she caused in European capitals and her reputation as a symbol of chastity and charity.

The portly showman's own reputation had already offended Americans, and was almost certain to offend an artist of Lind's tender sensibilities. At twenty-five he had leaped to prominence when he exhibited an aged and toothless negro woman claiming to be George Washington's 161-year-old nurse; when she died it was discovered she could not have been older than ninety. From this gross beginning he had gone on to mermaids, Siamese twins, midgets, Sioux Indians who turned out on close examination to be disguised actors, and other such varieties. At thirty-nine Barnum was a patron saint of promotion, his fertile brain bursting with ideas for attractions. His customers accepted bamboozlement because they were never sure that Barnum would *not* present the authentic wonders promised.

Brimful of enterprise, the promoter was in many ways a representative American of the times. The citizenry of the 1840s was ready to try any idea that looked as if it might be profitable, and the country teemed with ambitious men who made business into a kind of religion. Nobody was sure that they would not produce wonders. Many did. Between 1840 and 1850 the United States doubled its imports and its exports, ending the decade with more railroad mileage and more merchant ships than Great Britain, the richest country in the world. Americans sailed the fastest ships in the world, invented the telegraph, ether anesthesia, rubber-soled shoes, envelopes and air-conditioning, began using adhesive postage stamps, and danced the polka to demonstrate sympathy with revolutionists in Europe. They boasted about their "manifest destiny" and took over vast territories to prove it.

Despite this frenetic activity, leisure sat more easily on the American conscience during the 1840s than it had in earlier days, when "idlenesse" was "evil." Françisquy Hutin gave the first performance of ballet in New York in 1827, and every woman in the lower tier of boxes at the Bowery Theatre walked out in protest against her scanty costumes. But when Fanny Elssler arrived with her ballet company in 1840 she was given a banquet by members of Congress and a reception at the White House by President Martin Van Buren and his cabinet. Everywhere she appeared she was cheered and applauded.

Magazines and newspapers flourished, more books were read than ever before, and literary societies, museums, libraries and lyceums mushroomed. "America is a poem in our eyes; its ample geography dazzles the imagination," wrote the intellectual arbiter of the period, Ralph Waldo Emerson. The seer advised artists to celebrate "dramatic spectacles" in their poems and in their pictures, and he meant such subjects as clearing forests, planting crops and trade.

In the big cities, where there were increasing amounts of money to spend, Americans went on a pleasure binge. Shakespearean drama was favored theatrical fare, and so was melodrama done with the cast on horseback. Tyrolean and Swiss bell ringers and traveling orchestras were also popular, but no entertainment was attended more happily than a minstrel show. "They paint their faces black, sing negro songs, dance and jump about as if possessed, change their costumes three or four times each evening, beat each other to the great delight of the art-appreciating public, and thus earn not only well-deserved fame, but enormous sums of money," a disgruntled German musician wrote home to the *Neue Berliner Musikzeitung* in 1849. "Circus riders, rope dancers, beast-tamers, giants, dwarfs, and the like are in such numbers that they may surely be reckoned as forming a certain percentage of the population."

Few first-rate musical performers had traveled throughout the nation, and it was generally thought that their earnings would be meager if they did venture forth. In 1843, however, Ole Bull, a Norwegian violinist, created a sensation and earned substantial sums, subsequently invested in a 125,000-acre colony for Scandinavians in Pennsylvania named "Oleana." Two years later Leopold de Meyer, the first pianist of international reputation to visit the United States, arrived in New York. De Meyer was hailed in the press as one of the "wonders of the age." He sometimes played with all ten fingers, sometimes with thumbs alone, and sometimes with his cane, which he used to drum a variation.

In 1846 Barnum attended a concert given by Henri Herz, the second pianist of international reputation to arrive in the country. After the performance Barnum told Herz that he was thinking about a Jenny Lind tour of the United States, and asked him whether he might like to come along. The showman added that he would publicize Lind as an actual angel come down from Heaven.

Herz, no novice at hokum himself, declined the offer but asked incredulously, "You think you will make people believe that?" "They won't believe it at first," Barnum predicted, "but I'll say it and have it repeated everywhere so often and so well that they finally will believe it."

## 2. *The greatest musical wonder in the world*

Like Robert E. Lee seizing initiative during the Wilderness Campaign, Barnum grasped the possibilities of a Lind tour at once, pausing only to confirm intuitions.

When inspiration struck, the promoter was resting at Iranistan, his ornate minareted Byzantine-Moorish-Turkish home seventeen miles from the center of Bridgeport, Connecticut. He was brooding about his reputation. Barnum wanted a new public image for himself. He was tired of being thought of as a "mere" showman. Because he was a shrewd Connecticut Yankee, he was trying to think up ways to polish his image and to make some money, both at the same time if possible. He was considering a " 'Congress of Nations' . . . a man and woman, as perfect as could be procured, from every accessible people, civilized and barbarous, on the face of the Globe," when it suddenly occurred to him that a Lind tour could be undertaken at less risk, with less trouble and with greater profit.

For several days Barnum calculated costs on the backs of handy envelopes and thought about the tour. His deliberations led to two conclusions, later listed in his autobiography: "1st. The chances were greatly in favor of immense pecuniary success; and 2d. Inasmuch as my name has long been associated with 'humbug,' and the American public suspect that my capacities do not extend beyond the power to exhibit a stuffed monkey-skin or a dead mermaid, I can afford to lose fifty thousand dollars in such an enterprise as bringing to this country, in the zenith of her life and celebrity, the greatest musical wonder in the world, provided the engagement is carried out with credit to the management."

Barnum was not exaggerating when he wrote that Lind, who had studied with García's son, was at the "zenith" of her powers and the "greatest musical wonder in the world." Since 1846 she had enjoyed an unbroken series of triumphs, climaxed by recent appearances in London during which Queen Victoria tossed her a bouquet, the House of Commons could not meet three times because so many members were out paying her homage, and the aged Duke of Wellington followed her from concert to concert. Hector Berlioz said that her voice had "incredible agility, lending itself . . . to impassioned expression and to the most delicate ornamentation"; Chopin claimed that "the charm of her solo passages is beyond description." Mendelssohn wrote the soprano part of *Elijah* for her and said, "There will not be born in a whole century another being as gifted as she." But the composer also had to admit in bewilderment, "She sings bad music the best."

Musicians considered Lind a great singer, but to her Victorian fans she was more than an artist. She was a paragon of virtue and purity. She refused to appear in opera because opera was drama set to music, and the stage was "immoral." She detested the bohemian life, she contributed vast sums to charity, and her great ambition was to live near "trees, water and a cathedral."

Jenny Lind was homely, vain and moralistic, and Victorian concertgoers saw in her solid, shining qualities to be treasured. She had been born out of wedlock and reared by a harsh and neurotic mother who made her feel persecuted and unwanted. At heart she was frightened and embittered and suffered terrible feelings of inferiority that could not be completely assuaged by public acclaim. By 1849 she had been engaged to be married twice, and both times had been hurt emotionally when the betrothals were broken.

October 1849 was an opportune time for Barnum to entice Jenny Lind to tour for him because she was already contemplating a trip to the United States or to Russia, two countries where she thought vast sums of money could be earned. Though her gifts to charity were already substantial, she wanted to make a large donation to her favorite cause, a hospital for poor children in Stockholm. Russia was about to be ruled out because it was "like France" from a "moral" point of view, and France she considered "immoral." Besides, her companion, Mme. Josephina Åhmansson, did not wish to travel there. The United States was not like France and could afford even her fees.

While Lind was thus bemused, Barnum searched for an agent to negotiate with her. He chose John Hall Wilton, an Englishman currently in America managing a touring group called "The Sax-Horn Players." Barnum probably felt Wilton's qualifications as a musician and as an English gentleman would appeal to Jenny Lind. His instructions to Wilton were brief: Engage Lind on the basis of a share of the profits, if possible; if not, go to $1,000 per concert for a 150-concert tour. Wilton's earnings would depend both on his success in securing Lind's services and on the basis that he did so. If he did well for Barnum, he would get a "large sum"; if he failed he would get only his expenses plus a small fee for his time. Barnum furnished Wilton with letters of introduction to his London bank, Baring Brothers & Company, as well as to friends in England and France.

In November Wilton embarked for London, where he wrote Lind requesting an interview. She was resting in Lübeck, Germany, and refused to grant one. Wilton prevailed on Sir George Smart, conductor of the Philharmonic Society of London, to furnish a letter of introduction for him. This caused Lind to change her mind and she invited Wilton to Lübeck.

When they met, Lind was businesslike and frankly told Wilton that she was considering offers from three British managers and one American manager for a tour of the United States. The agent was nonplused by the news and forthwith proposed Barnum's top offer, $150,000 for 150 concerts, with no further attempt at negotiation. Lind also stipulated that she must be accompanied on the tour by Julius Benedict, a German conductor, pianist and composer who lived in London, and by Giovanni Belletti, an Italian baritone who was also a resident of the British capital. Wilton immediately departed for London to take options on their services.

While he was gone, Lind told his American competitor, Chevalier Wyckoff, about Barnum's offer. Wyckoff, who had managed Fanny Elssler's American tour and was an international playboy, retorted that Barnum was "uncouth" and a "mere showman." "Oh, what that man would not do! Why, that trickster would stoop to anything for cheap public display. He would not scruple, I assure you, to put you in a cage and exhibit you throughout the United States at twenty-five cents per head. Surely you cannot consider such a thing!"

Jenny Lind could consider such a thing but the warning troubled her, and she wrote Joshua Bates, a personal friend at Baring Brothers, asking for a character evaluation of Barnum. Bates assured her that Barnum had "character, capacity and responsibility" and would pay whatever he promised her. Earlier, she had also noted an engraving on a letterhead Wilton had used. It pictured Iranistan. "A gentleman who has been so successful in his business as to be able to build and reside in such a palace cannot be a mere adventurer," she had to admit.

Wilton returned after committing Benedict and Belletti to the tour but still was not able to persuade the soprano to sign an agreement at once. Jenny Lind demanded several stipulations. She must have control over the number of concerts per week and over the number of works she was to sing at each concert, provided they were not less than four. She was not to sing in opera. She was to have the right to sing at will for charity in each city, provided that at least two concerts under Barnum's management had been given before and she had consulted with him.

Finally, on January 9, 1850, Wilton persuaded the stubborn soprano to sign a memorandum of agreement. It committed Lind to tour under Barnum's management for a period of one year, if possible, or at the most eighteen months from the date of her arrival in New York.

Wilton hastened back to the United States to tell Barnum the news—there was no transatlantic cable as yet—and on debarking telegraphed the promoter in Philadelphia that Lind was his. Barnum had expected the negotiations would take longer and was startled by the message. A second reaction was concern that a premature announcement might wreck promotional plans. Barnum telegraphed Wilton to mention the contract to no one, and prepared to meet him in New York the following day.

Next morning, while the railroad cars were changed in Princeton, New Jersey, the happy, albeit secretive, promoter bought the *New York Tribune.* To his surprise, word had leaked out about the tour and the paper contained an account of the negotiations with Lind under the headline "Another Barnum Enterprise!" Barnum decided to make the best of a bad situation and learn how the public took the news. He told a railroad conductor who was an acquaintance that Jenny Lind "would surely visit this country in the following August."

"Jenny Lind!" exclaimed the conductor. "Is she a dancer?"

Barnum was chilled. If a conductor on one of the most traveled railroad lines in America could not identify the greatest musical wonder in the world, would six months be long enough to tell 23,000,000 other Americans about her?

### 3.  *A wonder and a prodigy*

Barnum, whose early career had included service as a house-to-house salesman, clerk, bartender, grocery-store proprietor, country newspaper editor, patent-medicine salesman and free-lance writer, thought the public a "very strange animal" even while he frazzled its nerves. "Although a good knowledge of human nature will generally lead a caterer of amusements to hit the people, they are fickle, and ofttimes perverse," he wrote. A slight misstep in management could spell disaster for the most promising enterprise, and he considered the Jenny Lind tour fraught with greater financial risk than anything he had yet tried.

How much more risk he learned from Wilton, who reported not only that Lind was to get $150,000 but that Benedict would earn $25,000 and Belletti was on the payroll for $12,500. In addition, and at Barnum's expense, Lind was to be provided with a maid, a male servant, a coach and horses with the necessary attendants in each city she visited, and travel and board expenses for herself, her secretary and Mme. Åhmansson. Wilton had also promised that the soloists' fees of $187,500 would be deposited in advance at Baring Brothers.

Barnum was undaunted. He "at once resolved to ratify the agreement" and went to a bank for a loan, offering his Jenny Lind agreement and some second mortgages as security. No, said the banker he faced, "it is generally believed in Wall Street that your engagement with Jenny Lind will ruin you. I do not think you will ever receive so much as three thousand dollars at a single concert." Barnum was indignant at the banker's "want of appreciation," and retorted that he would not take "as much as $150,000" for his agreement with Lind. Nobody offered it to him, and he went from bank to bank until he finally obtained a letter of credit for a large part of the deposit from the banking house of Howland and Aspinwall. He was still short, however, and it was only after he sold some real estate and borrowed $5,000 from a Universalist minister that he could make good on the deposit.

After meeting with Wilton, Barnum also addressed himself to an equally meaty problem, his plan "to prepare the public mind." Here the promoter had no need to borrow anything, his limitless imagination providing all resources. Nonetheless, Barnum was well aware that he needed all the publicity he could get for serious music and for Lind, neither of these familiar to the masses he hoped to attract. Because he was a careful organizer who seldom failed to weigh all possibilities in a promotional campaign, he exercised utmost care in choosing exactly the points to publicize. It is this thoroughness that sets him off from lesser contemporaries who were satisfied to dismiss advertising as a series of haphazard, unconnected public announcements.

Barnum was sure that he could rely on Lind's professional competence—musical authorities had praised her often enough—but it was her pronounced disposition for "extraordinary benevolence and generosity" that interested him and, he thought, would stir customers. Barnum was confident "multitudes of individuals" would buy tickets in praise of virtue, if not of music.

On February 22, 1850, Barnum began his promotional campaign with a statement published in all the New York papers and afterwards in papers throughout the country. Money, he wrote, was of little concern to him: "If I knew I should not make a farthing profit, I would ratify the engagement." What was of concern was Jenny Lind "whose vocal powers have never been approached by any other human being, and whose character is charity, simplicity, and goodness personified." In England, she had given more money to the poor than he was offering her for the tour and had sung gratuitously for ten times that amount at charity concerts. Barnum said that she had a "great anxiety" to visit America and also reserved the right "to give charitable concerts whenever she thinks proper."

After the statement, Barnum did not have to work too hard placing stories about Lind and her charitable nature. Despite the railroad conductor's lack of information, newspapers had already carried stories about her. James Gordon Bennett's *Herald* and Horace Greeley's *Tribune*, battling for New York readers with scoops about sex murders and business panics, had also followed her career with interest. Editors on both papers began to play up stories from foreign sources about her musical triumphs and her charitable gifts. Various publishers also began to bring out brochures about her life and devotion to religion. Barnum helped everybody by hiring a newspaperman in England to write one or two articles a week about Lind and to send them to New York via the fastest ships. These articles were datelined London and accepted without question as legitimate news stories by trusting editors.

On August 14, two and a half weeks before Lind and her troupe were due to arrive in New York, and when interest was already rapidly building to fever pitch, a letter, allegedly written by Benedict to Barnum, appeared in the *Tribune*. It heartened the promoter with news that Lind was singing better than ever, thanks to a "timely and well-chosen repose." Benedict also confided that Lind was "very anxious to give a Welcome to America in a kind of National Song" (a statement hard to accept since she was later reluctant to sing it). Benedict offered to compose a setting if a suitable text by "one of your first-rate literary men" could be found. Three days later, all the New York papers carried an announcement by Barnum that he would sponsor a contest for "such a song as may be accepted." Judges were already chosen, the deadline was September 1, and a prize of $200 would be awarded.

Seven hundred and fifty-three texts from poets throughout the United States and Canada were hastily mailed to Post

Office Box No. 2743 in New York, the address Barnum gave. The winning ode was written by a twenty-five-year-old poet, journalist and travel writer, Bayard Taylor. Some of Taylor's competitors later learned that one of the judges was his publisher and another a colleague at the *Tribune* office. They were much vexed by the discovery. Barnum was denounced in the press as a charlatan, but offered no excuses. He considered most of the contributions "doggerel trash," and was frankly pleased by the excitement. At a cost of $200 he reaped a publicity harvest including several hundred angry letters written to newspapers (which mentioned his name), and gained a solid reputation in the literary trade as a friend of poor but deserving newspapermen.

Meanwhile, Lind was in Sweden preparing to leave for New York. Barnum arranged for her to give some concerts in England while she was en route to America and hired a music critic to write reviews for a Liverpool newspaper. The critic's accounts of frenzied triumphs were rushed aboard a ship leaving before Lind's and reached New York in time to stir up even more advance interest. "Lind possesses a greater combination of greater excellence than all who have gone before her," claimed the *New York Morning Courier and Enquirer*. "It seems to be admitted, in fact, that she approaches as nearly to perfection in her art as can be expected of a human being unaided by magic power."

## 4. *Such enthusiasm*

Just past noon, on September 1, 1850—when church was out and New Yorkers could stroll down to dockside—the United States mail steamer *Atlantic*, with Jenny Lind and party on board, arrived off Manhattan. More than 30,000 rapturous potential customers jammed the dock and a dozen city blocks to catch a glimpse of her. Seven hundred firemen waited patiently to escort her to her hotel.

That morning Barnum, sporting a large bouquet, had been rowed out to the ship from Staten Island. The owner of the steamship company, however, reached Lind first with a larger bouquet. When Barnum was finally able to exchange greetings with Lind, she asked him when and where he heard her sing. "I never had the pleasure of seeing you before in my life," he responded. Bewildered, she asked why he would risk so much money with so little knowledge of what he was buying. "I risked it on your reputation, which in musical matters I would much rather trust than my own judgment," he replied.

Barnum had a coach waiting at dockside. After Lind's party fought its way to the vehicle he mounted the box and sat beside the driver, instead of sitting beside the artist. "My presence on the outside of the carriage aided those who filled the windows and sidewalks along the whole route in coming to the conclusion that Jenny Lind had arrived," he later wrote. Seated topside, Barnum also helped crowds identify Lind as his attraction. Shouts of "There's Barnum!" were mixed with cheers for Lind.

After the welcoming ceremonies Barnum was convinced that audiences would be much larger than he dared hope at first. So was Lind. Forty-eight hours after she arrived, he relates in his autobiography, he advised her that not only would she get $1,000 for each concert, besides all expenses, but "after taking $5,500 per night for expenses and services, the balance shall be equally divided between us." "Mr. Barnum, you are a gentleman of honor: you are generous . . . I will sing for you in America—in Europe—anywhere!" he says she replied—a touching portrayal of confidence unhappily suspect because of another version.

This one, by Maunsell B. Field, of the law firm of Jay and Field (which represented Lind in the United States on Baring Brothers' recommendation), has it that the artist left Europe without having signed a contract with Barnum. The day she arrived in New York, Lind asked Field to draw up a contract; the following day she met with Field and Barnum to discuss terms. Lind demanded that Barnum increase her fees over what Wilton had promised and agree to yet another stipulation that the contract could be terminated by either party after one hundred concerts, provided a forfeit was paid. This was Barnum's first experience with the side of Jenny Lind that was not angelic. "Whatever his motive, [Barnum] was most obliging and complaisant," Field was to write. "Although I have never since met him, I have always esteemed him for the good nature and liberality which he exhibited."

Barnum did not consider the increase "wholly an act of generosity." For one thing he was certain there was going to be enough money in the venture for everybody involved. For another, he wanted to forestall the possibility that "envious persons" would "create discontent in her mind." Moreover, he probably did not want to slow down the momentum of his promotional campaign with disputes. His next big publicity gambit, a public auction for opening-night tickets, was at hand.

The idea to sell tickets at an auction was not original with Barnum. Years before, he had attended a ticket auction for Fanny Elssler's dancing show in New Orleans. The publicity value impressed him as much as the cash receipts. Accordingly, six days after Lind arrived, he held the first of two auctions for opening-night tickets at Castle Garden, the hall selected for the debut performance. A crowd of more than 3,000 braved a rainstorm to come and bid.

The first ticket put up went to a local hatter named John N. Genin, whose Broadway shop was next to Barnum's American Museum. Newspapers from Texas to Maine reported the purchase to 2,000,000 readers, and residents and out-of-towners made it a point to buy a hat at Genin's shop, just to see the man who had paid $225 to see Jenny Lind. During the next twelve months, Genin sold 10,000 more hats than during the previous year. Disgruntled bidders muttered that Genin was Barnum's brother-in-law. This was not true, but Barnum did advise his friend Genin to buy the first ticket at any price.

By September 11, the date of Lind's American debut, it was clear, to quote Barnum, that "there had never before been such enthusiasm in the City of New York or indeed in America." All tickets had been sold at the two auctions, and New York's first ticket speculators had started in business. Jenny Lind Songsters, Jenny Lind Musical Monthlies, Jenny Lind biographies, Jenny Lind gloves, Jenny Lind shawls were on sale everywhere. Reporters assigned to the upcoming concert were hard-pressed to think of new superlatives to describe Jenny Lind. The *Tribune* brought a fresh music critic, John Sullivan Dwight, from Boston. The *Morning Courier and Enquirer*, afraid of gaffes by ribald enthusiasts, gave instructions how to behave at a concert. The *Herald* predicted the impression Lind would make: ". . . the voice and power of Jenny Lind . . . will far surpass all past expectations. Jenny Lind is a wonder and a prodigy in song—and no mistake."

## 5. *The sweet warbler*

When Jenny Lind stepped through the doors at the back of the Castle Garden stage at her first New York concert, an audience of seven thousand strong—mostly men—screamed, cried, yelled, cheered, hurrah'd, and tossed hats and bouquets into the air. Overhead, a bank of flowers, suspended above the balcony, spelled out the words WELCOME SWEET WARBLER. Julius Benedict and sixty New York musicians, who had begun the performance at 8 P.M. with the Overture to *Oberon* by Weber, waited to accompany her in the aria "Casta Diva" from Bellini's *Norma*. Earlier in the program nobody had paid much attention to them or to Signor Belletti's renditions. The preliminaries had served only to whet the audience's appetite for Jenny Lind.

The "Sweet Warbler" the audience saw turned out to be a plain, thick-featured woman, thirty years old, with black hair pinned back so tightly it flattened her ears, giving rise to the rumor that she had none. She was wearing a simple white dress. She curtsied deeply. Then she stood still because she realized that she would not be heard above the roar of approval that followed the curtsy.

Jenny Lind hated and feared crowds, and when she began to sing her voice wavered and reflected her nervousness. She slowly gained confidence. After she completed the selection, there was another tumultuous demonstration that ended with a shower of bouquets at her feet.

During the remainder of the program every selection Lind sang was cheered wildly. Every composition anybody else played or sang was merely tolerated. Outside the hall, a crowd of music lovers and toughs attempted to storm its way into Castle Garden. Only the determined use of police batons prevented a riot.

At the end of the concert, shouts of "Barnum! Barnum!" brought the promoter to stage center. The elated showman told the joyous throng that "Mademoiselle" Jenny Lind "herself begged [me] not to mention on this evening one of her own noble and spontaneous deeds of beneficence," the donation of her share of the evening's proceeds—$10,000— to charity. This was a signal for six more cheers, three for Lind and three for Barnum. Lind was not able to retire that night until the Musical Fund Society performed a serenade in appreciation for a $2,000 gift.

Next morning, reports Barnum in his autobiography, "the people were in ecstasies . . . I think there were a hundred men in New York . . . who would have willingly paid me $200,000 for my contract," but debut receipts were less than he anticipated. Several bidders had not picked up their $12 to $25 tickets, and the seats had gone unoccupied. Instead of $20,000, $17,864 was earned. This made Lind's share less than $10,000, but Barnum decided to divide the proceeds of the first two concerts equally between Lind and himself and thus allow her to make good on her promise.

After five more concerts in New York and gross receipts of $87,055, Barnum took Lind and her troupe to Boston, Philadelphia, Washington and other cities. There were no elaborate preparations for touring musical groups in 1850, and any trip was full of risks. Barnum arrived in a city, rented the largest hall, announced the dates and times of performances, and hoped for the best. In each community Lind received a noisy and lively reception, however, because Barnum always telegraphed ahead to an agent to make sure the citizenry knew she was coming.

In Washington, President Millard Fillmore, his cabinet, and most of Congress came to hear Lind sing. Ex-Secretary of State Daniel Webster arrived late at one of her concerts from a well-liquored party at the Russian Embassy, rose on his unsteady legs, and joined in the chorus of "Hail Columbia."

In Boston, the mayor hurried to the hotel where she was staying and told Lind and a crowd of voters, "It is not your superhuman musical endowments that have captivated our senses, it is your unblemished private character." Lind wondered out loud just what he knew about her private character. "Madam," responded the New Englander, "where there is so much goodness of heart as you display, there must be virtue."

In Philadelphia, Lind complained that she had a headache and could not wave to crowds in front of her hotel. Her bonnet and shawl were hurriedly thrown on Mme. Åhmansson, and Mme. Åhmansson was led out on a balcony. The crowd unknowingly cheered the companion instead of the artist.

In New Orleans, Lind was afraid to debark from the ship that had brought her from Havana, so great a crowd had assembled to cheer her. Barnum put a veil over his daughter's head and escorted the girl down the gangplank while his right-hand man, Le Grand Smith, shouted, "Make way, if you please, for Mr. Barnum and Miss Lind!" The pair fought their way to the hotel where Lind would stay. A few minutes later the artist was driven down quiet streets in a closed carriage to her hotel.

Ticket auctions became standard procedure in each city, always good for a story in local papers. In Boston, Ossiam M. Dodge, a vocalist, paid $625 for a ticket, and when Lind heard about it she said, "What a fool!" But all of Dodge's concerts were henceforth well attended, proving that he was not so foolish. In Providence, William C. Ross paid $650 for his ticket and then failed to attend the concert.

Jenny Lind was much annoyed by this type of publicity, using the derisive word "humbug" to describe it. Barnum liked to be called "Prince of Humbugs," a title he coined himself; he considered it necessary to pull at the public's heartstrings so that it, in turn, would loosen its purse strings. This character trait caused difficulties between him and Lind, who he found had an ungovernable temper and indulged in tantrums whenever she could not have her way. The tour was often punctuated by arguments between the two. Again and again she wanted changes in her contract to her advantage.

In May 1851, the Lind troupe returned to New York for fourteen concerts. Jenny Lind had achieved a greater success than anyone dreamed possible. Single concerts in New Orleans, Richmond and Cincinnati had each earned over $11,000, and a charity concert in Baltimore cleared more than $37,000. Barnum cut his advertising budget to a minimum while newspapers maintained a publicity drumbeat for him and photographers sold pictures of Lind everywhere.

Despite these triumphs, Lind's relationship with Barnum deteriorated. Chance advisors whispered that Barnum was just a "cheap" showman. John Jay, who took Field's place as her attorney, said that Barnum was "an albatross around her neck." Her secretary, who was plotting to become her manager, claimed that Barnum was earning more from the tour than his star, and as early as the sixtieth concert of the tour, in Memphis, Tennessee, pressed Lind to dissolve the contract.

After a concert in Philadelphia's National Theatre, the scene of an earlier circus performance, Lind indignantly told Barnum that she "was not a horse" and asked that their contract be terminated. Barnum was weary of sporadic arguments. After the ninety-third concert, in June 1851, he agreed to accept $1,000 for each of the remaining seven concerts in addition to the $25,000 forfeit fee previously agreed on to end his association with the artist.

Barnum then retired to the spires and minarets of Iranistan. He often went to hear the artist sing, but he was happy to forego business dealings with her and never tried to renew them. Over a nine-month period he had grossed $535,486.25 for himself and $208,675.09 for Lind. The average receipts per concert were $7,496.43. He was justifiably proud of these feats.

The decision to drop Barnum was a serious mistake for Lind. Business details bored her, and she was often a victim of chicanery. Her advisors proved to be poor managers, and she fired her conniving secretary and managed her own performances with her husband, a pianist named Otto Goldschmidt, whom she married in America. "People cheat me and swindle me very much, and I find it very annoying to give concerts on my own account," she complained to Barnum one evening. Her novelty was also wearing off, and without Barnum cast in the role of villain there was no one to blame for failures but herself. In Philadelphia, one paper heartily agreed with her decision to give no more concerts there. "She looked as stingy as a hive of wasps, and as black as a thundercloud, and all because the house was not crowded."

Lind gave her farewell performance at Castle Garden on May 24, 1852. It rained that day and attendance at the concert was good but hardly impressive. Receipts were less than half what they were at her debut. Many critics did not even bother to attend.

Barnum was sent a complimentary ticket, and after the concert he went backstage to bid the singer farewell and to tell her that she must never stop singing. "Yes, I will continue to sing so long as my voice lasts," she agreed wearily, "but it will be mostly for charitable objects, for I am thankful to say I have all the money which I shall ever need."

On May 29, 1852, Lind sailed for Europe on the same *S.S. Atlantic* that had brought her to America. That morning, New York's firemen, steadfast in their loyalty, presented her with a gold box and a copy of Audubon's *Birds and Quadrupeds of America* in a rosewood case. But in contrast to the 30,000 who had shouted hello, only 2,000 were on hand to wave goodbye.

## 6. *Elements which surprise the judgment*

Seven months after Jenny Lind left the country, *The New York Times* poked fun at the pretensions of "fashionable" music lovers and critics but felt that interest in Italian opera had an "eminently beneficial effect upon musical appreciation." Much of the credit for developing this interest was given to Jenny Lind. "Her concerts were so happily compounded of the differing elements, which surprize [sic] the judgment by startling ability of execution, or subdue the feeling by infinite pathos, that multitudes who had hitherto scoffed at foreign music, became devout and humble admirers thereof. Never have audiences so large, and so heterogeneous, been crowded within the same walls." The editor said that the public would no longer be satisfied with "money-craving academies of music" and remarked that to part for the last time from the "very loveliest of human voices" was a grievous experience. Almost overwrought, he prayed "Heaven bless Jenny Lind!"

The furor that Jenny Lind provoked did have beneficial effects on musical life in the country and undoubtedly sped the development of a general interest in music. Opera houses were opened in several cities. In New York, after four previous attempts to found a home for Italian opera had failed, the New York Academy of Music was successfully opened in 1854. Three years later an Academy of Music was opened in Philadelphia. In 1859 the French Opera House was opened in New Orleans, the scene of some of Lind's most successful appearances, and in 1861 the Brooklyn Academy of Music was opened. As far away as San Francisco there were Jenny Lind theaters.

News of the great sums that Lind had earned caused many European celebrities to consider American tours. Two of the greatest divas of the period, Marietta Alboni and Henriette Sontag, were busily touring the United States within months of Lind's departure, but these renowned artists were less successful than Lind. Aside from the fact that they did not have Barnums for managers, it was said disapprovingly that Sontag encouraged suitors to drink champagne from her slipper and that Alboni had as many lovers as Lind had charities.

The same standards did not apply to male performers. Much of pianist Louis Moreau Gottschalk's success—almost comparable to Lind's—was based on his fatal charms for female music lovers. Gottschalk wore white gloves when he came on stage and before performing removed them one finger at a time. Women rushed to the platform, tore the gloves to shreds and then fought over the pieces.

Barnum's rewards were professional as well as pecuniary. His reputation among fellow promoters and impresarios increased as much as his prestige with the public. He was paid the ultimate compliment of imitation by dozens of fellow practitioners. Typical is the campaign launched for Maria Piccolomini in 1858 by two impresarios, Maurice Strakosch and Bernard Ullmann. Like Lind, Piccolomini was generous. But there the similarity ended. A London critic remarked that when Piccolomini sang the role of Zerlina in Mozart's *Don Giovanni* "such virtue as there was between the two [Don Juan and his victim] seemed absolutely on the side of the libertine hero."

Piccolomini's innocent approval of all schemes gave Strakosch and Ullmann irresistible opportunities to pour forth an incredible array of messages, all ridiculous. The crafty managers whispered to reporters that the singer was a lineal descendant of Charlemagne and of Max Piccolomini, hero of Schiller's drama *Wallenstein*. These fantastic claims served merely to strain credulity. A ticket auction was likewise a failure. Yet the soprano's New York debut was a triumph, one newspaper reporting that the audience "literally botanized her with bouquets" and that she "vaulted at once into the affections of the audience. . . . The general public is charmed, fascinated, dazzled and led captive by her."

Nonetheless Barnum could not duplicate his own success. In 1853, as president of the Crystal Palace exhibition in New York, he sought to "unite in one grand ensemble the elite of the instrumental celebrities with the great choral societies, solo singers, etc., of Boston, New York, Philadelphia, Baltimore, Cincinnati, etc." There was too little interest in the plan, however, and it was abandoned. That year he offered Gottschalk a one-year contract and $20,000, but was dismissed by the pianist's father as a "learned showman of beasts." One result was that Gottschalk's earliest years touring the United States were unprofitable and unrewarding.

The promoter again took to the circus. Jumbo the elephant, Samson the bear, Jo-Jo the dogfaced boy, Wild West Shows—Barnum presented them all. In his later years he became as much of an attraction as his oddities. He first published his autobiography in 1855, and in 1869 published a "new and independent" autobiography, which watered down some of the franker details of hoaxes recorded in the earlier work. Thereafter he revised the book almost every year. Thousands bought it to learn the secrets of his success.

Modern writers still consider Barnum a showman rather than a musical pioneer. For all his pains, he remains the "ancient showman and cheapjack of the fairs reshaped to play upon the urban masses." Though the Jenny Lind tour created a market for serious music, Barnum has been heaped with calumny—mainly because he made the tour successful in a circus atmosphere bereft of a dignity that is supposed to be part and parcel of the art.

Elements of his showmanship have stuck to the artistic life. Barnum's philosophy of the indirect publicity approach (virtue and charity before music) has been used for a conductor's hands here, a soprano's recipes there. Historians see in the promoter's unholy union of press agentry and art the genesis of troubles that have since plagued the development of a serious audience for serious music.

And yet the tour remains a remarkable and unique achievement. Conceived by a promoter with no previous experience in serious music, supported by a public with no interest in serious music, it shook the nation into an enjoyment of serious music. It proved that America was ready to take a forward step in the arts. For this, P. T. Barnum deserves an important place in the annals of American musical history.

# II. *Cultivation of Taste*

## 1. *Art in all its ramifications*

NEW YORK had a population of 515,547 in 1850 and had "arrived at the state of society to be found in the large cities of Europe." Its social elite was second to none in display of worldly goods, but it still remained bereft of an opera house. Among those most affronted by this omission were the patrons of the late Astor Place Opera House, who had never given up hope for a new cultural adventure.

Since it was unthinkable to build another opera house in the Astor Place vicinity, where street gangs roamed, in 1852 the patrons resolved to build a new theater farther uptown, in the fashionable Union Square neighborhood on Fourteenth Street. Plans for the "New York Academy of Music," the name chosen for the new house, also called for a larger seating capacity and lower admission prices than had prevailed at the Astor Place Opera House.

Unchanged were the conditions under which New York's opera houses were operated. Impresarios would continue to take all the financial risks. For a stock subscription of $1,000, each patron got a share of rental income, a free ticket to each performance, and no responsibility for the overhead. The impresario who leased the hall got that.

To give the enterprise increased cultural tone, Academy directors applied to the state legislature in Albany for a charter. Suspicious lawmakers refused to grant one, on grounds that the house was merely a "commercial" theater. A revised application specifying "cultivation of taste by entertainments at moderate prices" and "facilities for instruction" was duly sent north, and on April 10, 1852, the legislators finally granted the charter.

At Horace Greeley's *New York Tribune* office on Park Row, William Henry Fry, dean of American music critics, was thrilled by the news. He speculated that "art in all its ramifications may [yet] be as much esteemed [in America] as politics, commerce or the military profession." Fry looked forward to a "golden age" of American musical life and claimed that the "dignity" of American artists was now "committed" to the hands of the Academy's directors.

Fry had no qualms about the patrons but many qualms about the promoters who would lease the Academy. Exactly what would they present? he wondered. If they wanted surefire hits they would engage European celebrities. If they wanted to "cultivate taste" they would probably lose money. Obviously, no promoter wanted to lose money. But then how would the glorious new Academy be different from a "commercial" theater?

This question troubled Fry, and in the spring of 1853 he cautioned Academy directors: "The Academy of Music should be above speculation. Its character should be benign and genial. If it be considered a platform for putting money in the pockets of the last adventurers from Europe, it will assuredly fail."

Fry's point was well taken, but directors, solid businessmen all, addressed themselves to more immediate questions: Who would take the lease and for how much?

In March 1854, Academy director James Phalen, a real-estate speculator who owned the lot on which the Academy would stand (and sold it to the corporation for $60,000) promised the lease to Max Maretzek for $30,000. Maretzek hurried to assemble a company. While he hurried, directors awarded the lease to James H. Hackett, an actor famous for portrayals of Falstaff, Rip van Winkle and Nimrod Wildfire. Hackett had ready cash, some experience managing plays, and a contract with the celebrated tenor-and-soprano husband-and-wife team of Mario, Cavaliere di Candia and Giulia Grisi.

Meanwhile, at Irving Place and Fourteenth Street, the Academy neared completion. The gilt-and-white building took nearly a year and a half to build and cost $275,000, "a sum much larger than was originally contemplated." Its builders boasted (mistakenly) that it was the largest "theatrical building" in the world. And as opening night—October 2, 1854—drew near, society was convinced that at last New York had a fashionable home for opera.

## 2. *Stockholders in a doubtful speculation*

Mario and Grisi were not well known in America but they had a great reputation in Europe, where a family of six children made for good Victorian public relations. Hackett had promised them $95,000 for sixty-three performances and deposited $50,000 in advance with Baring Brothers in London. Anxious to recoup his investment, Hackett rushed them to work almost immediately after their arrival in New York. Initial critical reaction was not uniformly encouraging. "Distance lends enchantment" was the best the *Musical Review and Choral Advocate* could say to readers.

The results of Hackett's unseemly haste were not fully apparent until opening night at the Academy, when it was discovered that 1,500 customers were on hand instead of the 4,600 the house was built to hold. Nor was this the only surprise. Because of the elegant auditorium's horseshoe shape, dozens faced pillars and hundreds faced each other. Worse yet, nobody could find a single room in the building set aside for "educational purposes."

"A giraffe could not see round some of the corners," said the *Times*, which thought the Academy was a triumph from "the acoustical point of view." The *Musical Review and Choral Advocate* despaired that "the most well-disposed friend of the association would wander vainly over the opera-house to find in any of its characteristics the justification of its name of Academy. The building is but an opera-house . . . those who have provided it for the public are but stock-holders in a doubtful speculation. . . ." At the *Tribune*, Fry offered up the hope that the Academy would yet become a "living truth" and not a showplace for the "vulgar adventurer from Europe, rich in the science of humbug."

The morning after the grand opening, Academy directors were in no position to figure out what a "living truth" was. If Hackett failed to make ends meet, directors themselves would have to underwrite productions, an appalling prospect. Hackett reduced ticket prices. For a month he did well. But in November his losses totaled $8,000. In December a director named W. H. Payne came to his aid. Together, impresario and director lost $4,000. On December 29, after forty-three performances, Hackett took a benefit performance for himself and quit the Academy.

In January, three months after opening night, the Academy was dark, and frantic directors offered the lease to every manager in New York. "Each of us," says Maretzek, "was willing to take the lease for a spring season after Lent or for a winter season from October 1855, but not immediately in the middle of the winter."

In February, the Academy was leased to Ole Bull, whose socialist colony in Pennsylvania, "Oleana," had gone bankrupt.

Bull's tenure was heralded by announcements that the Academy would become the "home of refined and intellectual amusement . . . an ACADEMY IN REALITY" and would also sponsor a contest for a composition by an American composer. Two weeks later the violinist said that he was $12,000 more in debt, and he abandoned the Academy. Maretzek had opened Bull's season conducting the American premiere of Verdi's *Rigoletto* ("[Its plot] violates every sense of poetic justice," groaned the *Musical Review and Choral Advocate*) and then presented Felicita Vestvali as Leonora in Donizetti's *La Favorita* (a "suicidal choice," moaned the *Albion*).

After seizing costumes and scenery for *Rigoletto* and two other new operas, *Il Trovatore* and *William Tell*, a committee of stockholders took the helm. Audiences for presentations were often sparse. In March, 250 people were on hand to hear a performance of *Lucia di Lammermoor*. In April, between 300 and 400 heard the American premiere of Rossini's *Stabat Mater*. A promised production of Fry's *Stabat Mater* never materialized after Phalen said that the management had "no prospect or expectation of making anything out of [*Il Trovatore*, and was] not willing to throw away money merely for the sake of gratifying the public and giving employment to some three hundred artists and supernumeraries."

Into this caldron of seething ambitions and disappointed hopes plopped a troupe headed by one of the renowned singers of the day, Anna Caroline de la Grange. Her company was scheduled to appear at Niblo's Garden, but an offer of more cash lured it to the Academy instead. The result of this base temptation was critical acclaim for the directors. "Our citizens owe them [the directors] a debt which cannot easily be repaid for presenting opera of the first class," said *Dwight's Journal*. But when Academy presentations finally came to an end in late July, the loss to managers and stockholders over the ten-month period from opening night was estimated to be $56,000, an appalling sum at the time.

But alas, during that first season, a pattern was set, one not to be altered until the arrival in 1878 of the intrepid Colonel James M. Mapleson. "Spasm opera," Fry called it. Constant change of managers was the rule. Maretzek, Maurice

Strakosch and his brother Max, and Bernard Ullmann, each took deficit-ridden turns. Like human windshield wipers they followed the same back-and-forth route, returning to the scene of earlier and disillusioning labors. "The payment of rent was scrupulously enforced," says Maretzek, "and if not forthcoming, the music, dresses and properties were seized and kept for half or one-third their value, and afterward rented out to the new lessee or manager."

## 3. *Refinement, intellect and culture*

No event created thornier problems during the early days of the Republic than President Thomas Jefferson's purchase of the Louisiana Territory from France in 1803. New Englanders feared that Southern states would establish slave empires in the new territory and that the agricultural South would overshadow the commercial Northeast. Some disgruntled Yankees even talked about seceding from the Union and forming a Northern Confederacy based on states' rights and strict interpretation of the Constitution, which had no provisions for the acquisition of foreign territory.

It was Jefferson's great personal popularity that decided the issue in favor of acquisition, but the President was handicapped by not knowing exactly what he had purchased. In 1804 he ordered two army captains, Meriwether Lewis and William Clark, to mount an expedition and to explore the huge uncharted territory. In December 1803, he had dispatched a general, troops from Ohio, Kentucky and Tennessee, and a civilian named William C. C. Claiborne to take possession of New Orleans, a port located 107 miles up the Mississippi River from the Gulf of Mexico.

Commissioner Claiborne began his official reconnaissance of New Orleans by counting up the buildings and the people in town. One finding was Le Théâtre St. Pierre, in St. Peter Street, which had been the site of performances of French opera as early as 1792. Another finding was the Creoles, a local aristocracy descended from French and Spanish colonists, who set the tone of New Orleans' social life. The Creoles were gay and sophisticated, and they considered Claiborne, who spoke no French, a hopeless boor. Their women shocked Puritan visitors by using rouge on their cheeks; the men fought duels at the slightest provocation. Both used the word "Américain" as a term of opprobrium and the word "Kaintock" (Kentuckian) to frighten disorderly children.

With remarkable stubbornness the Creoles resolved to keep New Orleans a French city, despite the American military and commercial presence. Contact with outlanders was limited by design, the populace looking to Paris for inspiration in food, fashions and music. But New Orleans was fated to be swamped by Midwesterners after the city became an outlet for Illinois lead, Kentucky tobacco, Missouri furs and other products.

Claiborne found New Orleans to have muddy streets, a sultry climate and an almost unbearable stench from garbage. Yet it enjoyed a gay reputation because of its masquerades and fancy-dress balls, which Creoles loved to attend. This reputation was enhanced in 1808 when light opera was produced at Le Théâtre St. Philippe, and it further improved in 1813, when a refugee from Santo Domingo named John Davis opened Le Théâtre d'Orléans on the site of a playhouse that had burned down.

Davis presented French plays and French light opera, and during the 1820s took his "Troupe Française de La N. Orléans" as far afield as New York, Philadelphia and Boston for performances. Some five years after it was opened, the Théâtre d'Orléans burned down, but Davis rebuilt, adding a wing called the Orleans Ballroom, which became famous for the Bals du Cordon Bleu, better known as the Quadroon Balls. These were popular entertainments for Creole men—it was there that mixed-breed mistresses were acquired.

Grand opera is said to have been introduced to New

Orleans in 1810, but it did not become a regular feature in cultural life until Davis's son, Toto, and an associate, Charles Boudousquie, began presenting regular seasons. Anglo-Saxons paid scant attention to the form, but Creoles immediately hearkened to the Théâtre d'Orléans. It became the one place in New Orleans where anyone with social pretensions had to be seen. "The display of beauty and exquisite taste in dress, on Tuesdays and Saturdays [the grand opera nights each week] were something positively startling to a stranger . . . ," reports a guidebook of the period. "Refinement, intellect and culture were visible on every side." Full-dress suits were also visible and were obligatory everywhere in the house but the parquet, the only section open to nonsubscribers.

Vulgar disturbances which marred presentations in the North were unheard at the Théâtre, where a set of city ordinances governed behavior. Anybody who made "a noise at . . . shows or theaters, whether by striking on the floor, the benches or boxes, or in any other manner" was liable to a twenty-five-dollar fine. On the other hand, the patience of audiences could not be tried by long intermissions; maximum time allowable was thirty minutes for the shifting of "grand scenery." Otherwise the interval could not exceed twenty minutes.

In 1851, Jenny Lind enjoyed one of the great successes of her American tour in New Orleans, a city opposed to almost everything she stood for. By this time New Orleans had acquired a reputation throughout the North as the "Southern Babylon," a city so steeped in revelry that Sundays were given over to faro and roulette. Travelers from New England thought that it even approached Paris in the sinful tendencies of its multitudes.

As in the French capital, duels were constantly fought over the merits of singers. Local impresarios were forced to become expert swordsmen. In 1859 Placide Canonge, then manager at the Théâtre d'Orléans, was challenged to a duel by Émile Hiriart of the *Daily Delta*, who did not approve a recent casting decision. Canonge was wounded and his friend Edmond Locquet took up his sword. But Locquet was even less able a duelist than Canonge; he was dispatched immediately by the critic.

At mid-century the leading local impresario was Charles Boudousquie, who had married the city's leading prima donna, Julia Calvé (no relation to Emma Calvé, of later and greater fame). In March 1859 Boudousquie's rent at the Théâtre d'Orléans was raised a few hundred dollars. Angered by the increase, the manager decided to build his own house, and he formed a stock company capitalized at one hundred thousand dollars. Boudousquie set a completion date in late November and was told by a prominent local architect that the deadline was ridiculous.

The manager hurried to see James Gallier, Jr., son of the renowned architect who had built the Pontalba Buildings in Jackson Square, the first apartment houses in the United States. Gallier said yes, his firm could finish an opera house by late November, and got permission from authorities to keep huge bonfires burning all night at the construction site so that work could go on around the clock. Yet it was only three days before opening night, December 1, 1859, that Gallier was able to tell Boudousquie that the French Opera House, the "lyric temple of the South," was ready for occupancy.

The house turned out to be a four-story plastered-brick building of Italian style that could hold 2,500 people on gala occasions but seated 2,078 comfortably. Nearly every seat afforded a view of the stage, and many thought it the best-designed opera house in the country. Almost immediately it served a social as well as a musical function; the French Opera House became a center for romance in New Orleans.

Creole girls sat prettily in family loges, not budging even during intermissions. This was because young men took the opportunity to stop by between acts and to chat—of course under close surveillance by chaperones. The girls tried hard to attract as much male attention as possible, since an empty loge was tacit admission that the young lady was only a "tapestry along the wall."

Boudousquie's first season was a social and musical triumph. His second season had barely started when he found himself without a star soprano. His wife, Julia Calvé, had retired from the stage. A replacement either jumped blithely on a chair and broke her leg or proved to have a poor voice—contemporary accounts differ. Faced with ruin, the manager engaged a slim, dark, Italian-American soprano, not yet eighteen years old, who was totally unknown in the city.

Adelina Patti had been "discovered" by Max Maretzek, who lived next door to the Patti family in New York. On the way to and from school each day she dropped by Maretzek's office and sang a "Jenny Lind favorite." Everyone within listening distance was struck by the incredible beauty of her voice. The moppet also stood on a table at a public concert when she was seven and sang "Casta Diva" from *Norma*, which she had heard her mother singing while cleaning the house. Critics hailed "Little Miss Patti" as the most astounding prodigy ever to appear in America.

Maurice Strakosch married Adelina's sister Amalie and became the youngster's manager, coach, personal representative and conductor. In 1860 he formed a partnership with his father-in-law for an Adelina Patti tour of the West and the South, to end in Mexico City, where she would join an opera troupe Maretzek was assembling.

The fateful meeting with Boudousquie occurred en route to Mexico City. Patti's first role at the French Opera House was Gilda in *Rigoletto* with Strakosch conducting. When she appeared on stage she received a polite welcome. A few minutes later, bravos began to be heard. At the end of the performance she received an ovation. Patti was to remain for three months of appearances.

Meanwhile, in Mexico City, Maretzek wondered what was happening. He found out after Strakosch sent him two telegrams. The first merely advised of a change in plan. A second bluntly reported that Patti would not travel to Mexico because she was afraid of its bandits. "Adelina and her Papa send you their best regards," Strakosch added.

Stranded in Mexico City without a prima donna, Maretzek devised a solution to his problem unique in the history of music. The impresario made roller skating popular. The skating scene in his production of Meyerbeer's *Le Prophète* was a sensation. Mexicans formed roller-skating clubs, each of which requested and paid for the privilege of allowing its members to glide across the stage during the appropriate part of the performance. Night after night the house was crowded while the novelty lasted. "The Gran Teatro Nacional," writes Maretzek, "became a well-paying skating hall with a performance thrown in as an added entertainment for the same price of admission."

In April 1861 Louisiana seceded from the Union, and there were only occasional performances at the French Opera House as 5,000 Confederates rushed north to defend Richmond from Federal armies. A year later, Admiral David Farragut and a Union squadron arrived off the mouth of the Mississippi and poured 17,000 rounds into two positions defending New Orleans, Forts Jackson and St. Philip. The bombardment was noisy but had discouragingly little effect on the fortifications. Farragut decided to run his fleet past the forts, and on April 24, 1862, the task force began a trip up the Mississippi that ended in the surrender of New Orleans.

The city was occupied by 15,000 troops under the command of General Benjamin Butler, a corrupt, walleyed Massachusetts politician, who, it is said, was not above stealing silverware. Butler was replaced, but in the interim New Orleans grew sick with hatred and violence. Riots were common; in July 1866, 40 were to be killed and over 140 hurt in disorders.

Despite unstable conditions opera quickly came back into fashion. In 1866 an Italian opera troupe performed in New Orleans and Creoles scraped up the money for tickets. This inspired the Alhaiza brothers to visit Paris and to recruit a troupe there to appear at the French Opera House. Marcelin

Alhaiza died in Europe, but his brother Charles decided to bring the troupe to America as planned. After debarking in New York, the artists boarded the *Evening Star* for New Orleans; 180 miles southeast of Tybee Island the vessel sank and nearly everyone aboard was lost.

There was public mourning when news of the disaster reached New Orleans. The Théâtre d'Orléans closed its doors. A month later the Théâtre burned down, and New Orleans was ready to resign itself to an opera-less season. At the French Opera House, however, the surviving Alhaiza brother, Paul, worked desperately, and finally assembled a troupe.

Such was the interest of the citizenry in opera that within a few years the French Opera House again became the home of one of the finest opera companies in America. The list of American premieres during the 1870s, 1880s and 1890s is impressive, including Thomas' *Mignon*, Lalo's *Le Roi d'Ys*, Massenet's *Hérodiade* and Saint-Saëns' *Samson et Dalila*.

Troupes from the French Opera House also toured the nation. There was considerable interest in New York during the 1892–93 season, when Oscar Hammerstein announced that he would present one. "Italian grand opera is all right but the Italian grand artists want the price of the earth to sing," he told a reporter, inferring that it would be more economical to hire French singers. Whether or not this were true, Hammerstein allowed the project to fall through, and the troupe never did appear in New York.

Around the turn of the century, the French Opera House fell on bad times and was allowed to deteriorate. Equally bad, attendance at the opera came to be thought old-fashioned, and the children of Creole aristocrats began to prefer other amusements. Each season cost a greater effort. Occasionally a season went by with no opera at all.

In 1915, the decrepit building was left in even worse condition by a devastating storm. A philanthropist named William Radcliffe Irby stepped forward, purchased the building and presented it to Tulane University. A sound thinker, Irby did not neglect to provide funds for the restoration of the structure.

At the end of World War I the French Opera House was again open for performances. An effort was made to make grand opera a part of the city's life, as it had been half a century before. It seemed as if the grace and zest, the elegance and character of the 1850s, as well as a building, might be restored.

On December 2, 1919, *Les Huguenots* was offered. Early the next morning someone saw smoke, and before much could be done to investigate, the entire house was ablaze. The stage, the curtain, the grand staircase were soon gone. Sixty-foot sections of the building came crashing down. New Orleans lost a glory that was never replaced.

## 4. *Of simple but imposing style*

Unlike New York or New Orleans, Philadelphia never completely lost its heart to Jenny Lind, but there was great ferment in the city for an opera house after her appearances. Philadelphians held to a quaint belief that the city was the social and intellectual headquarters of the United States, much as it had been in Federalist times. "There is afloat [in Philadelphia] an assumption of taste and criticism, savoring rather of those genteel discussions . . . of which we read in *The Vicar of Wakefield*," wrote Charles Dickens, who arrived for a lecture in 1842. But Dickens found the city's straitlaced appearance disconcerting: "After walking about it for an hour or two, I felt that I would have given the world for a crooked street."

At mid-century the Musical Fund Society, which was organized in 1820 "for the relief and support of decayed musicians [*i.e.*, indigents]" and "the cultivation of skill and diffusion of taste in music," was Philadelphia's leading musical organization. Its concerts drew fashionable adherents and yielded bounties for the poor, but were generally stodgy affairs. Attendance was not as good as attendance for performances by sumptuous opera troupes from New Orleans or New York. Moreover there was so much traffic outside the hall that music lovers had trouble hearing the Musical Fund Society Orchestra play.

Even before the New York Academy opened, a committee of socially prominent Philadelphians interested in hearing operas in peace and quiet advertised in two daily papers for the design of a new opera house "of simple but imposing style of architecture, the material of brick, with single or double walls." The house was also "to be arranged as to comfortably seat 4,000 persons in not more than three tiers of boxes, a balcony and parquet." And even before the $250,000 to build the "American Academy" was raised, two local architects, Napoleon Le Brun and Gustavus Runge, were chosen to design it. Excitement ran high when plans were announced, and in a frenzy of destruction preceding the construction the "Second" Chestnut Street Theatre, Philadelphia's leading playhouse, was torn down. Obviously it was no longer needed. But this later necessitated the building of a "Third" Chestnut Street Theatre when the Academy was found unsuited for plays.

The cornerstone for the Academy was laid in July 1855, and by December all that remained was to put on a roof, but for two years the brick building modeled after La Scala in Milan stood roofless. One reason was that the sponsors ran out of money, and the Academy ended up with 3,000 seats instead of 4,000. Another, less prosaic, reason is that Le Brun and Runge decided to let wind and rain temper the shell of the building.

Musically there was little to cheer about. The first season a native Philadelphian leased the Academy and then sublet to Max Maretzek, who opened the house on February 25, 1857, with a performance of *Il Trovatore*. In 1860 a special command performance for the future Edward VII was given

by Adelina Patti. But for half a century, until the advent of
Leopold Stokowski and the Philadelphia Orchestra, little of
national significance happened at the Academy except for the
American premiere of Gounod's *Faust* (in German) in 1864.
As before, Philadelphia relied on New York for its operatic
fare.

Much the same was true of the Brooklyn Academy of
Music which was opened on January 15, 1861. New York's
*Musical Review and World* dispatched a reporter to view the
festivities on opening night. He found that "in size it appears
to be a little larger than our Winter Garden. In fact, it looks
very much like any ordinary theater on Broadway, with this
difference, that we have seldom seen in any building of this
kind, such a profusion of red and brown colors. . . ."

Brooklynites incorporated their Academy in March 1859
"for the purpose of encouraging and cultivating a taste for
music, literature and the arts." The first opera scheduled for
presentation was *La Traviata*, but it was not performed until
1862. Protests about its "sinful" subject matter caused the
cancellation, and Mercadante's *Il Giuramento* was given instead. The following day, audiences heard the first lecture at
the hall, a practical description of horse-training methods during which several "vicious and refractory" beasts were exhibited.

The Brooklyn Academy had a stage almost equal in area to
the Covent Garden Opera stage in London and more than
a thousand gas jets revealing "the splendid proportions of the
house." But until 1903, when it was gutted by fire, it was
merely a convenient stopping point for opera troupes from
across the river.

## 5. *The Napoleon of impresarios*

Jenny Lind never traveled to California, but as far west as
San Francisco theaters were named for her and enlightened

citizens called for music and theater on a level with the "East," which was locally defined as the territory between Nevada and the Atlantic Ocean.

San Francisco, in 1850 the largest city west of the Mississippi, had a population of 40,000, and four hundred ships rotted in its harbor, abandoned by crews that had run off to the gold fields. Its inhabitants were coarse, vulgar and unprincipled. They hanged those fellow citizens that were considered unbearably depraved. Along the "Barbary Coast," dozens of dives and dancehalls featured seminude girls who provided the newest in dances and the oldest in professions. Leading citizens not only tipped their hats to the whores and madams, but often married them.

Seemingly mired in crime and harlotry, San Francisco was actually well on its way to becoming a metropolis. In 1850 it boasted four theaters, ten public schools, twelve daily newspapers, eighteen churches, a public library containing 3,000 volumes, and the world's best minstrel companies. The same year, Henri Herz, the first celebrated artist to visit the city, was presented at his debut with a pan of gold dust worth $10,000. The following year there were performances of French and Italian opera.

Frequent visits by musical celebrities were cause for much local pride. The *Alta California* boasted in 1853 that "There are probably few cities in the world, or any of its population, that afford so liberal a support to the same number of artists, of every class and order, as San Francisco." So far, so good. But "under such favorable circumstances, why is there not a movement made to establish here an operatic troupe of the first class, by subscription or otherwise?" asked the paper.

While editors awaited an answer to this question, Thomas Maguire, "Napoleon of Impresarios" by local repute, opened theaters in San Francisco and Virginia City and imported singers and dancers.

Maguire was a stocky, debonair impresario who arrived at the Golden Gate from New York in the fall of 1849. His first local enterprise was the Parker House, a combination hotel, saloon, gambling den and store, which regularly burned down. After each conflagration Maguire rebuilt. The fourth time he added a theater, the Jenny Lind. When the Jenny Lind went up in smoke, Maguire announced that a new, fireproof Jenny Lind would be opened. It was. And nine days later it burned down. A persevering sort, Maguire rebuilt a sixth time, importing yellow sandstone from Sydney, Australia, for Jenny Lind III, "The noblest and most imposing edifice in the state."

Jenny Lind III turned out to be a white elephant, and Maguire sold it to the City of San Francisco for use as City Hall. The sale precipitated a storm, many citizens wondering why $200,000 was paid for a building that originally cost $150,000. Maguire, whose friends in the political hierarchy made the sale possible, sat out the furor. The following year he took over a larger building, the famous San Francisco Hall of Minstrelsy, and renamed it the Maguire Opera House.

Maguire's avowed purpose was to provide San Franciscans with the best in entertainment. His most profitable presentations were minstrel companies led by E. P. Christy, Billy Birch and Billy Emerson. Grand opera was a personal passion that sometimes cost money. Still, the manager insisted on producing operas by Verdi, Gounod, Bellini, Donizetti and Rossini. Among the troupes he presented was the Bianchi Opera Company, the first to arrive in San Francisco complete with orchestra. San Franciscans were spellbound when the instrumentalists became silent, Bianchi hit his tuning fork, and a Paris Conservatoire "A" floated through the quiet.

Maguire's success on the West Coast led him inland to Virginia City, Nevada Territory, site of a silver rush in 1859 as wild as the gold rush of 1849 in California. Virginia City was near the great Comstock Lode. Its 30,000 citizens had ten saloons and one music store, Dale and Company, which stocked grand-opera scores.

Virginia City's wealth lured to it the same weird assort-

ment of prospectors, pioneers, adventurers, prostitutes, gun-
men and thieves as did San Francisco. They reacted badly to
musical programs strong in poetic content, much preferring
noisier demonstrations of musical competence. In 1864 violinist
Paul Julien was jeered for his soulful program. He decided
never again to give concerts on the Comstock. Virginia City
was mortified. Thirty-five leading citizens and merchants
signed an open letter berating the vile action of the rabble
and requesting the pleasure of hearing Julien play again. He
relented. At the second concert the audience was on its best
behavior, and the *Gold Hill Evening News* reported that it
"applauded vociferously during the entire evening."

Maguire's (Virginia City) Opera House was the town's
pride and joy. Seating 1,600 and with four private boxes, it
was considered fully representative of the community's grandeur and much superior to the opera house in San Francisco.
But there were deficiencies. On opening night, said the *Terri-
torial Enterprise*, a strong wind was blowing and caused
"considerable agitation" to the "fairer portion of the audience." The most "decided sensation" of the evening was that
produced on Mrs. Hayne, the leading lady, when a "shower
of gravel stones rained upon the building."

Such annoyances did not unduly upset patrons, and touring
opera troupes were popular, though the subtleties of *Il
Trovatore* and *Don Pasquale* often eluded auditors. "The most
exasperating defect we could perceive," said the *Gold Hill
Evening News* after a performance by the Brignoli Company,
"was the opera being given in Italian, of which our knowledge
does not extend beyond *poco tiempo* or *quien sabe.*"

In the middle 1860s, Maguire sold his Virginia City property
and centered his activities in San Francisco, where he was
promptly embroiled in a bitter war with the youthful but
dangerous de Young brothers, Michel and Charles, who had
recently begun publishing the *Daily Dramatic Chronicle*. The
impresario fired the opening gun by exiling their theatrical
critic from his houses because of an unflattering review. The

de Youngs were deprived as well of advertising revenues, and they printed lurid accounts of Maguire's public dealings and private life. Neither was able to bear close examination. The de Youngs also intimated in print that Maguire was personally responsible for a fire that destroyed the Metropolitan Theatre, his major competition.

Maguire sued for libel. Enraged by the suit, the de Youngs encouraged attendance at a new, luxurious house, the California Theatre, that surpassed both the Metropolitan and Maguire's (San Francisco) Opera House in lavish decoration.

Maguire lost the suit, but was awarded $32,000 by the courts in 1879, when the state legislature passed a bill authorizing street improvements that meant the destruction of his theater. Five years later he began the construction of a gorgeous $2.7 million palace to compete with the California Theatre. Financed by a well-known gambler, Elias Jackson "Lucky" Baldwin, it was called Baldwin's Hotel and Academy of Music and included 250 rooms and 18 shops in addition to the theater. Two years later, Maguire was dismissed from his position as manager, owing to losses of $50,000 on attractions. He embarked for the East and Europe, where he saw a new opera, Bizet's *Carmen*. "Just the hit of the century," he predicted, and on his return to San Francisco presented it, taking a loss of $20,000 in the process.

Though Maguire came up with new ideas for extravaganzas regularly, he had more and more trouble finding theatrical positions. He returned to Baldwin's in 1881 but was dismissed a second time, following the unprofitable engagement of an Italian tragedian. A benefit proferred by friends raised $1,500 for him. Maguire used the money to go to New York but returned in 1882 only to shake the dust of San Francisco from his feet for the last time.

The impresario's remaining days were spent in abject poverty in New York. A "Monster Testimonial" for "California's Pioneer Manager" at the Metropolitan Opera House in 1894 featured Nat C. Goodwin, David Warfield, Clara Morris and other stars, but Maguire received little money from it. Next year he was living on the charity of the Actors Fund in a run-down boardinghouse. When he died in 1896, scant notice was taken in the New York papers.

But in San Francisco theatergoers remembered his great triumphs. It was recalled that on one occasion he was anxious to manage a tour by the budding young humorist Artemus Ward. "What will you take for forty nights in California?" Maguire hopefully wired. "Brandy and water" was the reply.

# III. *A Novel Innovation*

Geselle ist, wer was kann;
Meister ist, wer was ersann;
Lehrling ist jedermann.

*Who knows his trade is a journeyman;*
*A master is he that invents the plan;*
*An apprentice, each and every man.*

      —*Motto of* C. F. Theodore Steinway

## 1. *Novel, ingenious and important*

So FASHIONABLE was music by the 1870s that many an American house was not considered a home without a piano. With lavish hand carving on its rosewood case, with mother-of-pearl keyboard, with solid-gold nameplate, a piano was almost divinely suited to Victorian interiors. To a couple setting up housekeeping, a piano was "only less indispensable than a kitchen range," the *Atlantic Monthly* reported in 1867.

There were those who scoffed at its popularity. "Every American woman feels bound to play the piano, just as she feels bound to wear clothes," wrote Xavier Eyma, a French reporter. Traveling up the Mississippi on a riverboat in 1860, Eyma found the instrument "inflexibly tortured from morning till night." Domestic newsmen were equally dismayed by excessive piano playing. The *Pittsburgh Evening Chronicle* decried "the adulation and toddyism lavished upon every Piano-Forte player of any talent [which] is enough to disgust all sensible people with the instrument forever. From the language of the musical critiques of the Eastern press, one would suppose that there was nothing else worth living for in this life but music, and Piano-Forte playing especially. . . ."

Two piano-manufacturing firms dominated post-Civil War America. In Boston, 500 employees of Jonas Chickering and Sons labored to turn out 2,000 pianos per year in a huge building said to be surpassed in cubic volume only by the national Capitol. In New York, Henry Englehard Steinweg, a piano maker who arrived from Germany in 1850, moved to a plant occupying an entire block front in 1860. For several years Steinweg manufactured nothing but square pianos. Then in 1859 came the first great Steinway invention, the overstrung grand that assured a gorgeous sound. In 1864 founder and sons signed a partnership agreement and the family had its name legally changed to Steinway. By the end of the Civil War the Steinways, like the Chickerings, were turning out 2,000 pianos per year.

Chickerings and Steinways alike took justifiable pride in the excellence of The Products, which in truth compared favorably with European wares. But it was victories over consumer resistance that kept factories humming, and great ingenuity was also exercised in the development of those stratagems that pushed sales figures upward. Doretta, Steinway's eldest daughter, sometimes offered free piano lessons to close a sale, but an early discovery was that a customer did not have to play a piano to buy a piano. It was enough that he could pay for a piano. By 1870, about one of every 1,540 Americans was doing just that every year.

Steinway and his sons, especially alert entrepreneurs, pioneered in advertising techniques, developing the use of the testimonial in the early 1860s. Steinway ads featured the names of local conductors and pianists who "personally examined and practically tested the improvement in Grand Pianos, invented by H. STEINWAY" and dutifully found them "most novel, ingenious and important." Despite the accolades, the Steinways were aware that testimonials from famous European virtuosi counted for more in the marketplace than did praise from domestic talents. In 1859 Henry Steinway, Jr., wrote his brother C. F. Theodore (who was making pianos in Germany) that Steinway and Sons was anxious to publicize its wares in Europe "in order to interest those piano virtuosi who come here [to the United States], so we'll get our hands on them."

The Paris Exposition of 1867 provided Chickerings and Steinways with an opportunity to go there to seize virtuosi; each firm is said to have spent $80,000 in its attempt to carry off top honors in the piano competition. Both were winners. Steinway and Sons took the first gold medal for the United States and endorsements from Berlioz and Rossini. Chickering and Sons also took a gold medal, and the firm got a testimonial from Franz Liszt.

In the early 1870s Steinway and Sons began the large-scale manufacture of uprights, popular in parlors. Henry and two sons lived in three identical brownstones adjoining the Steinway plant on Park Avenue, always ready to think about new ways to make pianos and to sell pianos. Steinway Hall, a four-story $200,000 structure which included showrooms, offices and a concert hall with 2,500 seats, was built on Fourteenth Street in 1866 to stimulate general interest in music, and particular interest in pianos. And in 1870 and 1871, a veritable duchy called Steinway was established on four hundred acres of Long Island, where Long Island City is located today. Complete with lumberyard, mill, foundry, public bath, homes for workers, free circulating library and school, Steinway was well organized, well governed and devoted, in the most basic sense possible, to pianos.

The spring and early summer of 1872 were hard days with plenty of unemployment in New York, however, and even the Steinways could not keep Steinway, Long Island, uncontaminated by a wave of labor unrest. In May, 500 of the city's 2,500 piano makers voted to strike for an eight-hour day which amounted to a 20 percent increase in pay. William, Henry Englehard's energetic third son, met with striking piece-workers in early June and said that he had "no desire to fight against the feeling of the Age." On the other hand, he had no desire to agree to an eight-hour day either. That would mean not only a raise in salaries, but also an increase in the price of a seven-octave square piano from $600 to $875. William predicted gloomily that any increase in price would result in a decrease in sales. He offered a compromise 10 percent raise in wages, and several workers accepted, to the consternation of strike leaders. By mid-June, after an attempt by diehards to seize the Steinway plant, the strike was broken.

This devotion to continued production with only moderate increase in price was typical of William, who had sat at a workman's bench himself. Born in Germany, William was destined to become president of Steinway and Sons in 1876 and to set up a land company, a streetcar line, a ferry line and a gas company, all to serve piano makers living in Steinway, Long Island. Such was his determination to move workers back and forth across the East River that he also promoted the digging of a tunnel which eventually housed the IRT subway tracks, and he served a term as chairman of the Rapid Transit Commission.

Even while the strike was on, William determinedly continued to think up ways to sell pianos. One problem along this line had been bothering the firm for years. Stated in its baldest form, the problem was that few buyers could tell the difference in quality between one piano and another. The public acknowledged that Steinway pianos were well built. Yet cheaper instruments with labels reading "Steinmay," "Stannay" and "Shumway" were often bought by befuddled customers unable to perceive appreciable differences between instruments. Prospective Steinway buyers were hoodwinked by shrewd salesmen, and the firm lost thousands of dollars each year in sales.

William reasoned that if a Famous European Virtuoso actually used a Steinway piano at public performances, the combination of excellences would be such as to make the name STEINWAY a permanent imprint on every prospective customer's brain.

William's choice of virtuoso was Anton Grigoryevich Rubinstein, a leonine Russian pianist who resembled Beethoven so closely that some thought him the master's illegitimate son. Rubinstein was already under contract for performances in North America and Cuba to Jacob Grau, an impresario noted for operatic presentations, and it was of Grau that Steinway made inquiries. On June 8, 1872, Jacob and his nephew Maurice signed another contract with the virtuoso. This agreement committed Rubinstein to a 200-concert tour of the United States under Steinway auspices to begin the following September. He was guaranteed $40,000, half to be deposited at a bank immediately.

Rubinstein had scarcely more faith in Steinway and Sons than did the striking piano makers. He trusted to a contract with all points neatly spelled out for protection against vagaries in the free enterprise system that the Steinways espoused. The pianist specifically enjoined the booking of any concerts in the "Southern States" (where he finally did perform) and "in establishments devoted to purposes other than artistic ones (at garden concerts, tobacco establishments [*i.e.*, cafes], etc.)." He insisted on protection from "savage Indians" and payment in gold francs at the end of the tour.

Twelve weeks after he signed the contract with Grau in Vienna, Rubinstein embarked for New York. He was to be the first major Russian artist to visit the United States, and in the spirit of later compatriots he conceived his trip to have educational as well as commercial purpose. He would introduce the music of Chopin, Schumann and Beethoven to America. His contract, Anton Grigoryevich thought, would protect him against those wild adventurers, the Americans.

## 2. *He ripped and he rared*

In 1872, Anton Rubinstein was forty-three years old, a titan of the piano, conductor of the Russian Imperial Court

Orchestra, a sophisticated man of the world. Maurice Grau was twenty-four years old, had worked for his uncle Jacob as libretto seller, office boy and advance agent, and was a recent graduate of the Free Academy (later City College of New York). Rubinstein was aloof, introspective, domineering and the founder of the bravura school of Russian pianists. Grau was a callow youth with a hustler's temperament, and was taking over management of the tour because Jacob Grau was sick.

The ill-matched pair quarreled constantly during a tour of the United States that stretched from New York to Central City, Colorado.

The tour began with a performance at Steinway Hall the evening of September 23. The audience packed the hall, overflowing to the steps outside. Rubinstein, heartily applauded as he came on stage, made a low bow "half to the audience and half to the nameplate of the piano." His major contribution to the program was his own D Minor Concerto, for which he was accompanied by the New York Philharmonic. At its conclusion, music lovers screamed, shouted, clapped, cheered and sent up flowers. The pianist gazed imperturbably over their heads. Rubinstein, it developed, was one of those artists who only grudgingly acknowledged vulgar displays of enthusiasm. He could sometimes ignore audiences completely, often refused to attend receptions and always rebuffed celebrity hunters.

After five concerts in New York, Rubinstein and a troupe consisting of Henryk Wieniawski, a violinist who accompanied him to America, two singers and a small instrumental ensemble embarked on the national phase of the tour. In Boston the pianist practiced continually, gave lessons and began to brood about his seven-concert-a-week schedule. It was dawning that this was quite a work load, considering that dates were scattered all the way to Colorado and back. "Damn many concerts," he predicted in a letter to William Steinway.

After Boston, Rubinstein's prediction became reality. Buffalo, Toronto, Montreal, Detroit and Cleveland flew by. In some cities he gave several concerts; in others only a single concert. "Each day I feel unhappier. I think often of breaking my contract. The tour has no end and becomes daily more difficult, more unbearable," he wrote William Steinway in a terse communiqué from Cincinnati. In Detroit, Rubinstein amazed Grau by learning some new pieces. "The moment he arrived in his hotel room, Rubinstein would begin to practice," wrote Grau. "How his constitution stood the immense strain is remarkable." In Europe, Liszt called the tour a "steeplechase de concerts."

Unnerved by the nightly seas of expectant faces and clapping hands, Rubinstein became quarrelsome. Wieniawski fell victim to his rages. In St. Petersburg the violinist had often failed to perform at conservatory concerts, pleading illness as an excuse. In America, wrote Rubinstein, "he was quite well and received for his tour 100,000 francs. . . . However ill he might be, he always contrived to find strength enough to appear on the platform with his fairy-like violin. The secret of his punctuality lay in the fact that by the terms of the contract he must forfeit 1000 francs for every non-appearance." Wieniawski, who lost a large part of his earnings in the failure of a New York bank, was incensed by such affronts and by the fact that he was cast in a supporting role. Never, he told newspapermen, would he have come to America if he had known he was merely to be hitched to Anton Grigoryevich's wagon.

There were frequent battles between Grau and Rubinstein. "Sturdy-minded," said the manager of the artist. "For a time I was under the entire control of the manager. May Heaven preserve us artists from such slavery," said the artist of the manager. Back in New York in December, Rubinstein announced to Grau that he must play a solo recital. Grau meanwhile had been working up plans for performances by "The Great Combination . . . and positively the last joint appearance of Rubinstein, Wieniawski and Theodore Thomas with his Unrivalled Orchestra." There was a compromise; the artist got a recital and the manager got "Great Combination" concerts. Grau tried to dissuade the pianist from giving a recital. The very word "recital" was just coming into American usage. Who, wondered Grau, would pay to hear a single artist perform?

"Great Combination" concerts, given at both the New York and Brooklyn Academies of Music in early January of 1873, were among the most ambitious musical enterprises yet attempted in the United States. With Thomas conducting the orchestra, Rubinstein played the Schumann A minor Concerto, the Beethoven "Emperor" Concerto and his own F major and G major Concertos, besides shorter works. Wieniawski also appeared on each program, playing favorites such as his "Polonaise" and "Légende."

On January 13, 1873, Rubinstein gave a recital at Steinway Hall. To Grau's surprise, receipts totaled $3,100, the highest of any Rubinstein performance to date. At a repeat performance in Boston, where Rubinstein's earlier concerts had been poorly attended, box-office receipts were $2,600, or $1,600 more than the troupe had taken in at any single performance there. Emboldened by the successes, Rubinstein made plans for a series of seven historical recitals, at which he would play nothing but esoteric works. "Do they accept this kind of program in Europe?" Grau asked anxiously. They were beginning to, responded Rubinstein.

In a brochure describing the series, Grau effused that the seven programs demanded "vast knowledge, herculean power, and unmatched skill." Only Anton Rubinstein could, he wrote, "venture on their consecutive presentation." Few disagreed; it seemed to *Dwight's Journal* that Rubinstein "wished in closing a most extended and laborious period of his concert career to put on record as the achievement of one man, what was never done before; namely, the performance . . . of the greatest number of important works by all the best composers."

And herculean the task was. Rubinstein traced the development of piano music with gargantuan helpings of composers from the Elizabethan virginalists on. The Beethoven evening included seven sonatas and lasted over two and a half hours, aside from encores. The Schumann evening was equally lengthy. The artist also made a point of playing the repeats in every composition by Mozart and later composers.

But even as the recitals called forth popular acclaim, they also highlighted Rubinstein's defects. One reviewer found it incredible "that one human brain should be able to remember so many intricate compositions, so as to perform them in rapid succession without the aid of notes . . . ," but was disappointed that the "interpretations [were not] of ideal perfection. It was evident that some of the selections had not met his eye for so many years that their general outlines alone were clearly remembered by him." The Chopin recital "was the most tantalizing of all the series. The hearer was continually plunged from the raptures excited by indescribable beauties, into absolute tortures produced by mechanical crudities of the most aggravating kinds."

In the commission of these sins, Rubinstein put on a better show than most pianists did playing the right notes. For years, a monologue entitled "How Ruby played" made the vaudeville rounds, describing for non-concertgoers just what happened at a Rubinstein concert. "Jed Brownin," the narrator in the monologue, was amazed when "All of a sudden, old Ruby . . . ripped out and he rared, he pranced and he charged like the grand entry at a circus . . . things got so bright and I hilt up my head. . . . He stopped a moment or two to ketch breath. Then he got mad. He run his fingers through his hair, he shoved up his sleeve, he opened his coat-tails a little further, he drug up his stool, he leaned over, and, sir, he jest went for that old pianner."

Rubinstein's "pianner," a Steinway, bravely withstood his pounding. He proved, if further proof was necessary, that it was an instrument of unquestionable strength, built to take even his fortissimo passages. It was "unexcelled by any [instrument] in the world," he announced at a farewell dinner in New York.

Grau earned faint praise. "The receipts and the success [of the tour] were invariably gratifying," Rubinstein wrote years later. "But it was all so tedious that I began to despise myself and my art. So profound was my dissatisfaction that when several years later I was asked to repeat my American tour, with half a million dollars guaranteed to me, I refused point blank." Rubinstein acknowledged that tour earnings "laid the foundation of my prosperity." He performed 215 times and went home on May 24, 1873, with $20,000 more than he had been guaranteed. Henceforth the popular American image of a touring artist would be a short, muscular, long-haired introvert who moodily wended his way from town to town with a Steinway piano.

### 3. *A traveling advertisement*

News of the Rubinstein-Steinway triumph made for glad tidings everywhere but the offices of rival piano manufacturers. In Boston, the Chickerings were particularly distressed. During the fifty years between 1823 and 1873, 41,000 pianos passed from Chickering salesmen to customers satisfied that they were buying the very best. Gottschalk had been a Chickering artist. Now all was threatened: the names Steinway and Rubinstein were linked together eternally in a combination of glamour and excellence that inspired confidence and moved pianos out of warehouses.

Chickering and Sons' top strategists pondered the lessons of the Steinway-Rubinstein foray. In 1875, after two years of pondering, the Chickerings announced a two-pronged attack, suspiciously similar to the Steinway and Sons effort: the firm would open a concert hall in New York (there was already a Chickering Hall in Boston) and would sponsor a tour by Hans Guido von Bülow, a German pianist who had turned down a Steinway tour offer in 1864.

Field commander for the Chickering task force was Bernard

Ullmann, who had managed Henri Herz's concerts thirty years before. In an advance barrage the Chickerings announced that the tour was being made by "popular" demand. "Rubenstein's [sic] remarkable tour through the states served only to increase the popular desire to see and hear von Bülow," claimed the Chickerings. This enthusiasm led to Chickering-von Bülow talks. Unlike the Steinway-Rubinstein talks, they were initiated at the pianist's request. The "pioneer firm" merely "understood" that "the eminent maestro had determined to use Chickering pianos for his public recitals." Such was the paucity of ideas among the Chickerings that it also took von Bülow to suggest that he "inaugurate, on or about the middle of October their new and beautiful music hall now erecting on Fifth Avenue."

There was at once a basic flaw in Chickering plans: Hans Guido von Bülow was probably the worst choice possible for a public-relations role. Intelligent and immensely talented, he was also egoistic, dictatorial, pathologically anti-Semitic, haughty, antagonistic and bitingly sarcastic. He was a short, thin, bald pianist with a scraggly beard who was apt to argue with almost everybody about almost anything. He was a bundle of woes still reacting, in 1875, to a trauma inflicted when his wife, Cosima, ran off with Richard Wagner, his friend and idol. Even before the von Bülows parted, Wagner had fathered a child by Cosima, whom the pianist had thought at first to be his own. Von Bülow also had several eccentricities. Drum playing, he maintained, soothed his nerves. Also, he would appear on stage for afternoon recitals holding a high silk hat, which he carefully placed under the piano before he began to play.

Torn between love and hate for his wife and Wagner, von Bülow was desperate to leave Germany in 1875. He seriously considered settling permanently in America (where an "easy fortune" could be made) or Russia (where he liked the ballet and belles-lettres). Von Bülow corresponded with Ullmann for years, and turned down offers to head conservatories in

Milan, Vienna and Paris, as well as in St. Petersburg, before he embarked for the United States.

On October 18, 1875, the pianist made his debut in Boston Music Hall. "In every case he gives you the infallible true reading," wrote one critic. "We were hearing Beethoven, as afterward Chopin, far more than we were hearing Bülow [but] he plays more from the head than from the heart. The effect produced *from him* [sic] is not precisely the inspiration of genius." A week later, von Bülow gave the premiere performance of Tchaikovsky's B flat minor Concerto, which had been dedicated to him.

Verdicts in the press were not wholly favorable to the concerto, but this may have been due as much to the pianist's style as to the work's modernity. In Russia, Tchaikovsky took equal interest in good and bad reviews of the concerto after this and other American concerts. "Think what healthy appetites these Americans must have," he wrote a friend. "Each time Bülow was obliged to repeat the whole finale of my concerto! Nothing like that happens in our country!"

Von Bülow's success seemed assured. After five concerts in Boston, *Dwight's Journal* was sure that no "promise of the coming season [can] be expected to surpass or hardly rival them in interest. They have been admirably managed; the programmes have put the noblest compositions of great masters foremost, if they have dealt also with the wild sensational products of the modern school, which at any rate please curiosity by showing to what marvelous perfection the finger virtuosity is carried." Chickering pianos also came in for praise: ". . . we believe all who have heard them will agree with us [that they] surpass anything we have ever heard anywhere in power, rich sonority, sweetness, evenness of tone and action, and which indeed have proved adequate to all requirements of such a master in such music and (strange to say) in such a Hall."

Von Bülow proceeded to New York, where he opened Chickering Hall with an all-Beethoven concert. "My first [performance] in New York was *tout simplement* the most colossal success of my career as virtuoso and, as my excellent manager says, the greatest triumph which he has experienced in twenty years," he wrote his mother. "In every respect civilization in the United States has arrived at such a state that I find Europe more than a half-century behind, and steeped in medieval barbarity."

Alas, the period of good relations between Hans Guido von Bülow and the United States did not endure. Some German-Americans had the audacity to question the master's Beethoven readings; worse, many of them liked to drop in at saloons and drink beer. Von Bülow told a *New York Sun* reporter that remarks about his playing were "beer criticism," and loosed a flood of invective at his compatriots. Angry protests flowed in from prospective customers.

Stunned by this flank attack, the Chickerings were totally unprepared for a frontal assault in Baltimore. During a rehearsal, von Bülow pulled the large wooden sign reading CHICKERING off the side of the piano (where it was regularly placed), threw it to the floor and shouted, "I am not a traveling advertisement!" During an intermission he hooked the sign back on the piano and proceeded to kick it vigorously.

The tour was terminated after 139 of the contemplated 172 concerts were given.

## 4. *Pernicious contracts*

Despite the von Bülow fiasco, no self-respecting manufacturer could be without concert managers and traveling artists by the 1880s. Chickerings and Steinways imported pianists each season; many lesser giants such as William Knabe and Company, the Weber Piano Company and the Everett Piano Company also took the field, motivated by urgent needs for sales. Firms staggered each other with rival virtuosi. The main criterion observed in importing a talent was the scope of his piano-selling popularity; if his performances boosted sales, they were considered good.

It was an open secret that no European pianist would come to the United States unless he had a guarantee from a manufacturer. "Pianists who have done their utmost to fit themselves for the service of Art . . . now find themselves in the incongruous position of mere advertising agents for the manufacturers," an irate contributor said in the pages of the *Atlantic Monthly*. "The fault, no doubt, lies with the pianists themselves who enter upon such engagements. And yet the yearly income of only too many American pianists would be seriously affected for the worse if they did not make these very pernicious contracts with manufacturers."

Some pianists switched manufacturers in mid-course in hopes of getting a better deal. There was Teresa Carreño, who went from Weber to Steinway to Everett. There was Josef Hofmann, also a precocious tyke, who went from Weber to Steinway. In between, the New York Society for the Prevention of Cruelty to Children compelled his father to terminate further concertizing until the boy was of "proper age." Peter Ilyitch Tchaikovsky endorsed the Knabe piano to get traveling money from St. Petersburg to New York, where he conducted opening concerts at Andrew Carnegie's new Music Hall. He then said that he liked Steinway pianos. Rafael Joseffy made a splendid impression at his Chickering Hall debut in New York in October 1879 and then joined the Steinway roster. In 1888 a mellower von Bülow was back, this time for the Knabe Piano Company.

A persistent problem for manufacturers was the pianist who gave simultaneous testimonials. Mr. Sebastian Bach Mills could play only one piano at a time but found that he could easily endorse two at a time. Ostensibly a Steinway pianist, he bestowed warm words of praise on Decker Brothers' instruments. Steinway and Sons told of the abuse in the *Music Trade Review*. Decker, they maintained, had "no other chance of having his grand pianos played in public by a first-class artist, except by paying the compensation out of his own pocket."

A worse case was Adelina Patti, a Steinway endorser who helped sell a grand piano to Charles Gounod in Paris in 1888. The following year Patti jumped the fence into the W. W. Kimball Company pasture. "It gives me great pleasure to testify to the merits of the New Kimball Piano," she said. "It has a wonderfully sweet and sympathetic tone and supports the voice in a most satisfactory manner." Into the Kimball catalogue went Patti's crucial words together with praise from Lillian Nordica, Minnie Hauk, Lilli Lehmann and Pablo de Sarasate, all of whom found merits in the Midwest instrument heretofore undetected by Eastern musicians.

Sales of Kimball pianos zoomed. In New York, Marc Blumenberg, editor of the *Musical Courier*, charged that the Patti endorsement was a forgery and thereby precipitated a quarrel between East and Midwest that went on for years. Periodically Blumenberg let loose a blast; periodically Patti issued glowing praise for the Kimball piano. Eager for ammunition, Blumenberg involved the Chickerings in attacks: "The statement made by Chickering agents in Omaha to the effect that Kimball also supplied Ernest Nicolini [Patti's husband] with a tub of Chicago spaghetti per day is not founded in fact," he reported. Never did Blumenberg retract or relent. This gave rise to a rumor that "powerful Eastern interests" were behind his attacks on Kimball. These "interests" were never identified, but must have been surprised when Blumenberg praised Kimball, calling him the "Napoleon of the musical instrument industry."

Steinway and Sons began a slow withdrawal from this morass of charge, countercharge and guarantee when it sold Steinway Hall in 1890. Its ads began to feature the names of royalty. Nicholas II of Russia, Wilhelm II of Germany, Queen Victoria and 174 aristocrats were all said to have Steinways in their palaces.

It was then that Steinway acquired the most popular pianist

ever to appear in America, one whose face and name graced Steinway ads for forty years.

## 5. *We have heard them all*

"We hear you have had brilliant successes in London and Paris," Charles F. Tretbar, a Steinway and Sons concert manager with a handlebar mustache, told Ignace Jan Paderewski by way of greeting in November 1891. "But let me tell you . . . you need not expect anything like that in America. We have heard them all, all the pianists, all the great ones, and our demands are very exacting." The thirty-year-old pianist, just arrived from Europe, silently debated taking the next ship back. A $30,000 Steinway and Sons guarantee for eighty concerts kept him stateside. "We also have here pianists of big reputation and remarkable talent and importance," Tretbar continued. "Their demands are modest because they know that piano music is not as well rewarded as singing or even violin playing."

As yet, Paderewski was not of big reputation. His 1888 Paris concerts were his first real triumph, and they had led to appearances in London in 1890, where George Bernard Shaw found him "an immensely spirited young harmonious blacksmith, who puts a concerto on the piano as upon an anvil. . . . Paderewski is at least exhilarating; and his hammer-play is not without variety, some of it being feathery, if not delicate." True, Paderewski's career started rather late. At the age of twenty-four he was just beginning three years of study with Theodor Leschetizky in Vienna. The eminent pedagogue would cry, "It's too late! It's too late!" while teaching him, and possibly despaired of developing anything great in this determined Pole who was always practicing, but who still peppered the air with wrong notes.

Tretbar was as despairing a believer in the pianist's box-office appeal as Leschetizky was in his musical abilities. "Owing to the extraordinary demand for reserved seats it has been decided to reserve the entire balcony," read Tretbar's ads for Paderewski's November 17, 1891, Carnegie Hall debut, but free tickets were given to anyone who promised to attend. Counting box-office receipts after the concert was not especially joyful: they totaled only $500. When the reviews appeared next morning there seemed to be few compelling reasons for attendance at forthcoming Paderewski concerts. "He began by disappointing some of his auditors," said the *Times*. "He is not the ideal pianist."

Another critic considered the concert a success, however, and put the onus for difficulties on Tretbar. The concert, he said, "was dangerously well advertised. Had he [Paderewski] failed to satisfy the expectations which had been aroused among the musically inclined people of New York his failure would have been nothing short of disastrous to his future in this country and a woful [sic] humiliation to his manager."

While everybody was reading the reviews, Paderewski was busy practicing for a concert the following evening. He had hurried immediately to his hotel after the debut to prepare for a performance that might well mean the difference between success or failure in America. A knock on the door stopped the music and announced the embarrassed hotel manager. Older guests at the Windsor "would not tolerate music at night," he said. Paderewski shouted, "Get your coat!" to his secretary, and the two rushed down to the Steinway warehouse on Fourteenth Street, where the pianist practiced until dawn. At 10 A.M. the very same morning he promptly (if sleepily) began a rehearsal with Walter Damrosch and the New York Symphony Orchestra at Carnegie Hall. Scorning rest, he returned to the warehouse after the rehearsal, repeating passages over and over almost to concert time.

By evening, dull rote had woven its magic. Paderewski's second concert was a sensation. "The success of Ignace Jan Paderewski is assured," read a *Times* headline next morning, a deduction proved right at a third concert, at which $3,000 was taken in at the box office.

The quick swing from defeat to victory took Tretbar and William Steinway by surprise. The manager hastily added eighteen concerts to the tour itinerary, but of six forthcoming performances in New York only one had been scheduled for Carnegie Hall. Madison Square Garden Hall, a small auditorium, had been chosen for the others. "Now, this is the end," cried Paderewski after the first performance in more intimate surroundings. "I shall break the contract, but I will not play again in that small hall." The pianist was not going to see a cash customer turned away because there were too few seats. "You are under contract and you will have to play in the hall that we have already arranged for," snapped Tretbar with that special friendliness that warmed his relationship with Paderewski. The dispute was aired before Steinway who ruled that the series should be shifted back to Carnegie Hall.

Paderewski's subsequent career was proof that the way to Carnegie Hall is practice, practice, practice. It was also proof that gimmicks can help. Hugo Görlitz, the pianist's secretary and later business manager, began early in Paderewski's American career to give fifty free tickets per concert to students, on the condition that they rush to the platform after a performance and cheer the artist. His idea of a rush to a platform was similar to General Phil Sheridan's idea of a Union cavalry charge against Confederate breastworks. The students must appear "overcome with a mad desire to get a nearer view of Paderewski performing his magic." Until the New York Fire Department made him stop, Görlitz continued staging rushes down main aisles of New York concert halls.

The union of press agentry and genuine dynamism being irresistible, Paderewski was catapulted to the front rank of virtuosi, a golden-red-haired, intense, magnetic, glamorous musical giant in the eyes of public and intelligentsia alike. Henry Finck, critic of the *New York Evening Post*, held up publication of his book, *Success in Music and How It Is Won*, after Paderewski's earliest appearances so that the pianist could write a chapter on "tempo rubato" for it. William Mason who, like Tretbar, had heard them all, compared him favorably with Liszt. Richard Watson Gilder, editor of *Century Magazine*, then one of the most influential periodicals in America, invited him to soirées where other guests included Mark Twain, Rudyard Kipling, Augustus Saint-Gaudens, Henry James and Eleonora Duse. Some knew Paderewski to be important, but did not know exactly why. In Texas the state legislature cheered him wildly when he entered the legislative chamber. Then an eminent lawmaker rose and beseeched him to favor the assemblage with a song.

Steinway and Sons geared operations to Paderewski tours, providing pianos on which he performed in his inimitable if erratic fashion. Paderewski arrivals in New York from Europe were grand parades to the Steinway warehouse, where seven grand pianos awaited his personal inspection. Of these, three were chosen for his personal use and dispatched ceaselessly to concert halls throughout the nation to arrive at least ten hours prior to performances.

Well aware of the public-relations role he was expected to play, Paderewski also dispatched himself to and fro in style. A private railroad car with kitchen, bedroom, chef, butler, masseur and physician moved him from place to place. His wife and her aides came along, as did such facilities for amusement as would while away the hours when practice could be forsaken. Poker was a favored pastime, and games were interrupted only for concerts. It all added up to a special pungent identity that was never duplicated, the private railroad car becoming as much a Paderewski trademark as the golden-red hair.

If he lived in the grand style, Paderewski also earned in the grand style. During his first season he grossed $95,000, and this was a season so badly managed that Tretbar was selling concert dates for as little as $200 and $300. During his second season, playing fewer concerts, he grossed $180,000, and the fourth season after his debut, 1895–96, he is said to have *netted* $300,000. Thereafter, his earnings seldom dropped below $250,000 a year. In one season, 1922–23, they were $500,000. Altogether he is believed to have earned $10 million, probably making him the highest paid concert pianist of all time.

Like a reigning king, Paderewski distributed largesse, and as his earnings rose, so did his contributions. In 1892 he played a benefit concert that earned $4,275 toward the construction of the arch in New York's Washington Square. Four years later he set up a fund of $10,000 to be used for prizes for American composers. The total proceeds from concerts he gave between 1914 and 1918 were set aside for war relief in Poland, and in 1932 he played a benefit for unemployed musicians at Madison Square Garden that earned $33,500. On a more grandiose scale, he spent $100,000 in 1910 to erect a colossal statue of the Polish King Jagiello, who defeated the Teutonic knights in 1410.

Not always did the spirit of benevolence extend to Steinway and Sons. After a quarrel with one of the Steinways, Paderewski repaired to the Aeolian Piano Company for two seasons while the Sons gnashed their teeth in bitter and collective defeat. When the Sons got him back, the bond between artist and manufacturer was made stronger, and even the pianos began to reflect the close association. Artur Schnabel was heard to complain that Steinway pianos were "terribly loud. These steeds," he averred, "are of the Paderewski breed, not made to canter in my paddock."

As advancing years signaled the decline of a pianism none too strong to begin with, Paderewski still continued to hold his public in thrall. Audiences everywhere advanced en masse to the platform to demand encores, some touching the piano in the hope that thus would they obtain the magical powers that animated the pianist. Dozens went to Vienna to study with Leschetizky. Women lined up to bid Paderewski hello, to bid him farewell, to urge him to return, to cause him to strain his right hand writing autographs and to buy Steinway pianos. At the White House, President Theodore Roosevelt was so affected by the famous Paderewski élan that he began shouting "Bravo! Bravo! Fine! Splendid!" without giving Paderewski a chance to finish playing the composition.

There were also those not so awed by the personality that they had no reservations about the pianism. At the height of his popularity, in 1905, Richard Aldrich of the *Times* acknowledged that Paderewski's "well-remembered qualities exercised their spell upon the most fastidious listener as of yore," but why was it all so noisy? "Some of the pounding that he did yesterday was scandalous. . . ." The same defect was noted by the same reviewer in the same place, Carnegie Hall, in 1907, 1913, 1917 and 1922. Throughout his career, listeners at a Paderewski concert could not be guaranteed all the notes written by a composer, but those they did hear were often unbearably loud.

Customers meanwhile bought pianos in unprecedented numbers; Paderewski's career coincided with a peak of sales activity during which manufacturers were richly rewarded for promotional ploys. In the spring of 1892 business was so good that there was serious talk among leading piano manufacturers of forming a piano trust, to be capitalized at $50 million. Five million dollars was set aside to buy out those firms that would not join, but the financial crisis of 1893 prevented the scheme from becoming a reality. The panic did not permanently affect the market for instruments. A high point was not reached until 1909, when 364,200 pianos moved off assembly lines. Thereafter the rate fell until 1931, when 50,900 units—a little more than 14 percent of the high figure—were manufactured. After the depression, lost ground was never completely recovered.

About 1910, Steinway and Sons, unquestioned leader in quality instruments, gave up its concert bureau. Pianists were well aware of the virtues of the Steinway piano. Ten years before, the Steinways had turned over their advertising problems to N. W. Ayer and Son, of Philadelphia. "Keep everlastingly at it," was the senior Ayer's motto, and that's just what he did for Steinway, repeating over and over again that the Steinway was "the instrument of the immortals," "the one supreme piano in the history of music" and "the inevitable preference wherever great music is understood and esteemed."

Out for the carriage trade, Ayer also concentrated on proving that Steinway and Sons was superior to petty considerations such as money. A 1905 advertisement bears the headline "Commercialism is the bane of the times," and the copy goes on to say that "all branches of business have been permeated by this national disease." Happily, Steinway and Sons stood "for higher ideals than mere gain." The ideals turn out to be "grandeur . . . power . . . ideal beauty of tone and . . . perfect mechanism." Not to be outdone by crass claims by rivals, however, Steinway admitted in a 1906 ad that "122,000 satisfied purchasers" had invested "upwards of $100,000,000" in The Product over a fifty-three-year period.

Beginning in the 1920s, Steinway and Sons commissioned oil paintings of artists who had performed on their pianos, and these pictures also found their way into Ayer advertisements. A favorite was Paderewski and a Steinway, both outdoors while a storm threatens. Another shows an intent Anton Rubinstein peering over the shoulder of Josef Hofmann, an equally intent moppet studying a score. Rubinstein can also be seen playing before a czar, and old Henry Englehard Steinway can be viewed puttering around his workshop. In 1927 came a tour de force in which a piano was not even shown: the first four-color, double-page advertisement in *The Saturday Evening Post*, a Steinway promotion, pictures Tristan and Isolde.

Though Steinway and other piano manufacturers still make capital of the fact that great artists use their instruments (and acknowledge the fact in advertisements and on concert programs), they have settled down to a sedate middle age bearing few traces of a once flamboyant and extravagant youth. No longer do scouts from piano companies search the concert halls of Europe for "traveling advertisements." But the artistic contribution of the piano companies during the heyday of the testimonial was an important one. If not for Steinway and Sons, Anton Rubinstein might never have come to America, and if not for Chickering and Sons, von Bülow would probably not have given the world premiere of the Tchaikovsky B flat minor Concerto in Boston. And if the piano had not been indispensable to a well-decorated parlor for at least three generations, how many would have had the opportunity to sample the masters at first hand?

# IV. *The Food of Love, the Lot of the Caterer*

*"If music be the food of love, the lot of the caterer who furnishes such refreshment to the public is not the less full of anxiety and annoyance, and managerial enterprise in musical matters is not a whit less liable to end in disaster."*

—COL. JAMES HENRY MAPLESON

## 1. *The bright side of things*

THE EARLY CAREER of James Henry Mapleson, the most flamboyant impresario of the nineteenth century, included studies at the Royal Academy of Music in London, appearances as a violinist and a singer, managerial training at Her Majesty's Theatre in London and service as a volunteer in the Honourable Artillery Company. Mapleson lavished promotional talents on British audiences from 1861 on, on American audiences from 1878 on, and on artillerymen whenever he had the opportunity; some of the most joyous tributes to his verve and efficiency are found in letters written by career officers.

"Colonel" Mapleson was a tall, handsome, mustachioed impresario with a well-starched shirtfront, whose most distinctive characteristic was his great optimism. He tried hard to see the bright side of things and made it a point not to think about business when he was away from the office. His outlook was refreshingly different from that of the brooding professional usually found in the field.

News of this buoyant impresario first reached New York in 1868. *Dwight's Journal* reported that three millionaires, "Messers Belmont, Stebbins, and Jerome . . . mean to import the well-known impresario Mapleson . . . ," but Mapleson did not set out to reconnoiter North America until January 1876. In quick succession he visited New York, Chicago, Philadelphia, Boston, Cincinnati and "other places." He returned to England convinced that Her Majesty's Opera Company, which he managed, would tour America the following year.

He was overoptimistic. It was in 1878 that Her Majesty's Opera Company came to New York, and the tour was born to such grief as few tours have known. En route from London to Queenstown, the port of embarkation, the impresario planned to "recruit the exchequer" by giving performances. Neither of his prima donnas (Etelka Gerster and Minnie Hauk) was known to the Irish, however, and slight acquaintances left Hibernians indifferent. Mapleson was forced to cable his United States representative for two thousand pounds, which arrived the very morning the group was to leave for New York. A new problem developed when the 140 artists demanded payment in gold. It was almost evening before the hardy manager was able to pay his singers and to move them on board ship.

Arrived in New York for presentations at the Academy of Music, Mapleson noticed that Etelka Gerster had "scarcely been her usual self," but attributed her low spirits to a slow recovery from *mal de mer*. Two nights before the debut performance he was responding to a toast at a banquet when physicians advised that Gerster had typhoid fever. "This was indeed a great blow to me," he writes, but since the news was received outside his office he decided not to worry about it.

Next day Mapleson announced that Minnie Hauk would sing the role of Violetta in *La Traviata* in Gerster's stead. This announcement gave rise to further complications. Giuseppe Del Puente, a baritone, refused to appear with Hauk. Another baritone, Antonio Galassi, was hurled into the breach. This had happy consequences: Galassi was a sensation.

Thus launched, Mapleson's troupe sang the grandest works

of the French and Italian repertories, among them *Faust, Don Giovanni* and *Robert le Diable*. When she recovered, Gerster was a sensation in *La Sonnambula*. The novelty of the season was Bizet's *Carmen*, hailed nearly everywhere, but not in the *Times*, where it was found "neither very good nor very original" and indicative of the bad taste of the period.

Busy in New York, Mapleson also presented a troupe at Her Majesty's Theatre in London. Costumes, properties, singers and a ballet master were shuttled back and forth across the Atlantic. Occasionally communications broke down. The manager cabled London for a "2nd tenor," and in Great Britain it was believed that a shipment of two tenors was wanted. One tenor was kneeling on the dock in New York, thanking God for his safe arrival, when Mapleson drove up and "requested him to re-embark at once." The despairing wretch had just enough time to return to London for a performance of *Lucia di Lammermoor*.

In December 1878, Mapleson and his American company boarded an "elegantly decorated" train for a seven-city tour. Everywhere they enjoyed success. In Boston, a performance of *Lucia di Lammermoor* brought forth Henry Wadsworth Longfellow and earned $7,000; 1,100 miles away in Chicago, customers stood for hours patiently waiting to buy tickets. A performance of Bellini's *I Puritani* was so crowded by Midwesterners that Mapleson summoned the mayor of the community to urge "upwards of a thousand people to leave the building."

Piano manufacturers entreated the celebrities to bestow praise on their wares. Steinway and Sons supplied free pianos to the entire company and received a useful letter from it expressing "unqualified admiration." In Philadelphia, agents of the Weber Piano Company invaded the hotel where the troupe was staying, removed Steinway pianos placed there and rolled in Weber pianos. Appraised of the raid, Steinway agents hurried to the hotel. At first sight of the opposing force, each side unscrewed legs from its respective pianos; after a brief battle Steinway agents were put to rout. That night Mapleson's fickle company made merry at Weber Piano Company expense, and the following morning new letters were signed attesting to the superiority of Weber pianos. But Mapleson's troupe had yet another deceit to perpetrate: before it returned to England its members publicly hailed the Haines Piano Company.

Mapleson's troupe returned to New York from national labors to begin yet another season of opera at the Academy on February 29. Again, all representations received tumultuous approval. Academy directors proferred Mapleson a three-year lease, to begin the following October. So confident and successful an impresario had never before been seen at the Academy, in New York, in the nation.

In America he had managed 164 opera performances and 47 concerts; simultaneously he had managed 135 operatic performances and 48 concerts in Great Britain. The Colonel was deluged with praise; an interview with him was a front-page story in the *Times*. At their departure for Europe in April, Colonel Mapleson and his troupe were serenaded by a band. In gratitude his chorus sang back the "Grand Prayer" from *I Lombardi*. But as the ship pulled away from the dock it was found that several performers had been left ashore.

## 2. *Those who laugh*

During the 1879–1880 season, Colonel Mapleson's second at the Academy of Music, a Vanderbilt, probably Mrs. Marie Kissam Vanderbilt, the Commodore's daughter-in-law, tried to rent a box. She was refused because no boxes were available. Loath to yield either to chance or to fellow customers, Mrs. Vanderbilt told her husband, William H., to do something. William H. did something. He founded the Metropolitan Opera-house Company, Ltd., and put the Academy of Music out of business as New York's opera headquarters.

The Vanderbilts knew that the mere offer of a premium could not move them from orchestra seats to box seats. William is said to have offered thirty thousand dollars for a box, and all he got in return was a haughty refusal from the Academy establishment. In 1880 the Academy favored old families (*i.e.*, with fortunes earned before the Revolutionary War), and were scornful of the Vanderbilts, the Morgans, the Huntingtons and the Goulds, whose fortunes dated from more recent times. The "Knickerbocker gentry" took the greatest delight in turning down newcomers; the newcomers seethed with boxless humiliation season after season.

As early as 1877 it had been rumored that William H. Vanderbilt would donate land at Forty-Third Street and Madison Avenue for an opera house. The death of Vanderbilt's father, Cornelius, and a subsequent family squabble over the legacy undoubtedly held up plans. In 1880 the Vanderbilts urged fellow have-nots to help construct a new opera house and to end the symbolic humiliation. Alert to the threat of competition, Academy directors called for a friendly parley with dissidents. August Belmont, the Academy's president, suggested that twenty-six boxes could be added to the Academy, but this sop was not deemed acceptable. On April 7, 1880, G. H. Warren, a Vanderbilt representative, announced to the press that $800,000 had been subscribed for the construction of a new opera house; six months later, Josiah Cleaveland Cady, a New York architect, was asked to design the Metropolitan Opera House.

At the Academy of Music, a spokesman named Kingsland scoffed. "The singular part," he said, "was [that] a huge number of boxes [would] be subscribed for in advance by wealthy gentlemen and owned by them. . . ." He found this ludicrous. The *Tribune* reported that "Those who laugh at the whole enterprise" claimed that the Academy "lost as much as $10,000" every year. "What ground was there for believing that a building costing, according to the announcement, about $2,000,000 could ever be made to pay?"

The question how the building could "be made to pay" also plagued the operatic pioneers. "No opera house in the world has ever paid as an investment, and none ever will," said James Roosevelt, a Met director. Fellow directors thought to make up deficits with rentals, and plans were altered to allow for income-producing units (shops, apartments and studios) on the premises. Less sanguine directors wanted to go even further and to drop the whole opera house idea. Their thought was to build a solid income-producing unit, an apartment building, on the site. Construction costs had gone up since the first flush of enthusiasm in 1880 and each director had been asked for additional help. Few were overjoyed. It was only by dint of a narrow majority at a board meeting in 1882 that the capitalization was increased.

The decision made to move ahead, it became necessary to award a lease to someone who would actually present opera. (At *his* risk, of course.) Ernest Gye, impresario at Covent Garden in London, was approached, and he gave Metropolitan directors a detailed description of Covent Garden operations. He was then passed up for a local entrepreneur, Henry Eugene Abbey, of Akron, Ohio, and New York, New York.

Abbey, a "magnificent and honorable gambler in stars," had played cornet in an Akron band, had taken out a road company when he was twenty-four and, in 1880, engaged Sarah Bernhardt for her triumphal American tour. The manager earned $100,000 and a national reputation. He skyrocketed to prominence just in time to be noticed by Metropolitan directors.

There was only one hitch. Ingenious, intrepid Henry E. Abbey knew nothing about opera. He was a "puissant personage" who had to hire someone to manage his company. A partner, John B. Schoeffel, could only grumble about costs, and possibly knew even less about managing a troupe than Abbey did.

Abbey's choice for legman was Maurice Grau, now thirty-three years old. Since the Rubinstein tour, Grau had managed opera and operetta companies; along the way he had also lost several fortunes. In 1876 Jacques Offenbach found him "twenty-eight but . . . seems to be forty; incessant work, cares of every kind . . . have aged him before his time. He has been in a business which is more feverish, more absorbing in America than anywhere else."

Immediately he was chosen and had chosen Grau, Abbey began to cast about for stars for his Abbey Grand Opera Company. The inimitable Adelina Patti was one target. Mapleson also sought the diva's services. Patti played off Abbey against Mapleson, forcing her fee up and up; eventually it was to reach $5,000 per performance (always payable by 2 P.M. the day of the representation) plus a percentage of box-office receipts over $7,500. The Colonel was the victor. "Colonel Mapleson comes here when he wants me to sing," she once explained to a New York newspaperman, "and he calls me 'My dear child,' and he goes down on both knees and kisses my hands, and he has, you know, quite a supplicating face, and it is not easy to be firm with a man of such suavity of manners."

Mapleson also reenlisted Gerster and the capable, experienced members of his Academy troupe. With these forces he felt ready and able to fend off troops from the Vanderbilt opera citadel. The impresario repaired to Europe for rest and contemplation, convinced that he would enjoy total victory.

While he was gone, Abbey lured away most of Mapleson's capable, experienced Academy opera troupe by offering higher fees.

To *his* complete roster Abbey now added such notables as Christine Nilsson, Marcella Sembrich, Zélia Trebelli, Emmy Fursch-Madi and Sofia Scalchi. He purchased costumes, scenery, and appointments for his troupe with no thought for expense. "Every costume, every shoe and stocking came from Worth in Paris," reports Lilli Lehmann.

In October 1883 New York was braced for a head-on collision between Mapleson at the Academy and Abbey at the Metropolitan.

## 3. *A successful issue*

One hundred and twenty-two boxes in three great tiers held Vanderbilts, Drexels, Whitneys, Harrimans and Huntingtons at the Metropolitan Opera House when Henry E. Abbey opened its doors for the first time on Monday evening, October 22, 1883. The opera was Gounod's *Faust* (with Christine Nilsson as Marguerite and Italo Campanini as Faust), and the performers thrilled the audience, but it was the combination of "largest opera house in the world" and millionaires that impressed reporters, who had heard both artists in the same work under Mapleson's management. "A grand temple of music," the *Times* called the Met. "[Millionaires] perfumed the air with the odor of crisp greenbacks," said the *Dramatic Mirror*. "The tiers of boxes looked like cages in a menagerie of monopolists."

The same evening Colonel Mapleson held forth at the Academy with Etelka Gerster in *La Sonnambula*. Mapleson's audience included Astors, Belmonts, Beekmans and Schuylers. They were gorgeous in their finery but fewer in number than the gentry at the Metropolitan.

Whose spectacles to attend? The question perplexed society for weeks. Performances were given by both managers on the same nights. Abbey presented *Faust, Lucia di Lammermoor, I Puritani* and *La Sonnambula* in succession. Mapleson countered with *La Sonnambula, La Gazza Ladra, La Traviata, Aïda* and *Faust*, which featured a new sensation in the role of Marguerite. The lady's name was listed in the program as Lillian Norton-Gower, but she later changed it to Lillian Nordica after her first husband disappeared upwards (in the most terminal sense) in a balloon ascension.

Almost immediately the impresarios were in financial trouble. Abbey's costs were $7,000 per night before the curtain went up; his receipts were less than $3,000 a night when the curtain came down. Mapleson writes that sometimes he took home for himself of an evening $22 or $23. During the "Patti nights" the Academy was two-thirds full; during the "Gerster nights" it was two-thirds empty.

As the 1883–84 season reached mid-point in December, both managers were hard pressed for cash and made plans to recoup losses via national tours. The Abbey Grand Opera Company opened first in Boston, on December 26, with Nilsson in *Faust*. "She has an incomparable physique, superb voice, admirable carriage . . . but she has faults . . . ," said the *Transcript* critic, a hard-to-please Harvard man named William Foster Apthorp. Abbey and Mapleson gave performances in Chicago at the same time. Through some logistical mischance, Patti, Gerster, Nilsson, Sembrich, Fursch-Madi, Trebelli and Scalchi —the *crème de la crème* of both troupes—were quartered on the same floor of a hotel. "Our condition of mind," said the *Inter-Ocean* contemplating the performances and the sopranos parked together, "is not unlike bewilderment at being confronted by the most famed of the world's sopranos. . . . The occasion was a triumph of music over every other consideration."

But the triumph of music was not complete. Mapleson was acclaimed for presenting Patti and Gerster and denounced for the weakness of his ensembles. Abbey was denounced for the "unworthiness, the outrageous shabbiness" of his settings and acclaimed for presenting Nilsson and Sembrich. For so true a believer in display as Abbey to be niggardly with settings is surprising. The virtue of thrift had never before occurred to him, but on this tour he committed the singular error of leaving his expensive stage sets in New York. Abbey used what he could find on the road and lost a major selling point.

From Chicago the Abbey troupe journeyed to St. Louis and then to Cincinnati, where flood conditions prevailed. Mapleson canceled performances in Cincinnati when he learned that waters were reaching record heights. This last decision proved costly for local sponsors, who had paid out nearly $3,000 for advertising, tickets and additional lights hooked up to the City Hospital gas supply. Sitting out the deluge in Chicago, Mapleson offered to organize a benefit for flood victims. His thanks was a line in the *Cincinnati Enquirer:* "Mapleson will be eternally damned."

Abbey arrived in Cincinnati just as flood waters reached their peak, but his company played to packed houses. While the crisis continued, customers lined up for tickets; as the waters receded, customers began to stay home. The streets dried out too fast, and Abbey's deficits mounted alarmingly. At the end of the two-week season the sponsoring committee turned down his proposal for yet another week of "festival" opera.

Mapleson was meanwhile reaping a lush crop of problems with Gerster and Patti. In Chicago, a performance of Meyerbeer's *Les Huguenots* featured Gerster as the Queen and Patti as Valentine. After the first act, in which the Queen's part is bigger than Valentine's, Gerster was deluged with flowers. Patti received only a single bouquet. The greatest musical star alive stood by helplessly as a rival enjoyed the crowd's favor. Patti screamed and kicked in her hotel room after the performance until she was forcibly put to bed. Morning brought no peace. Convinced that Gerster had the "Evil Eye," Patti refused ever again to appear on stage with her. Like many another Patti vow, this one was broken. But from this performance date Patti's and Gerster's constant departures from, and rejoinings with, Mapleson's troupe.

Abbey's financial condition deteriorated badly as he moved his troupe back East. "It oozed out," smirked Mapleson, "that prior to the entry of [Abbey's troupe into] Cincinnati, he had dropped on the road some $53,000." From Cincinnati the Metropolitan troupe traveled to Washington, where a series of performances was cut short for lack of interest, and to Baltimore, where Sembrich created a furor but only Nilsson brought out audiences. An engagement in Philadelphia had the unlucky distinction of earning the lowest gate of the entire tour, $700.72.

In New York, newspapers estimated Abbey's losses at $500,-000. It later developed that they were mistaken. Losses were nearer $600,000, a deficit of such magnitude as to astound even Abbey. Shrewdly the impresario offered to manage an opera company at no fee the following season, if Metropolitan directors paid his debts. Shrewdly the directors refused his proposition but offered him the use of the house for a benefit. "I beg also to express my hope that the results of the benefit may in some measure be commensurate with the manner in which you have presented Italian opera and to say that it will give me great pleasure to do anything I can to aid in making the benefit a great success," Edmund C. Stanton, secretary of the Metropolitan board, wrote the impresario.

For this last desperate attempt at solvency on April 21, Abbey put all his singing stars on stage. Two additional Abbey artists, Ellen Terry and Sir Henry Irving, appeared in a scene from *The Merchant of Venice,* and Marcella Sembrich enchanted the audience by playing the violin almost as beautifully as she sang. *Prime donne* went into the audience to take up a collection. The efforts of these artists enabled Abbey to pay off $16,000. It took him five years more to pay off the remaining $584,000 in debts.

While Abbey was working his way East, Mapleson was headed West to San Francisco, where crowds waited impatiently to hear his troupe. On his return to New York, exhausted by weeks of hard campaigning, he expected Academy directors to invite him to a banquet at Delmonico's "in recognition of the energy and skill with which, through unheard-of-difficulties, I had at last conducted my season to a successful issue." What he got was a terse reminder from the secretary of the Academy board that unless he made good on a loan from directors his belongings would be seized. "I felt sadly injured," he confesses, "at their sending the Sheriff in on the very night of Patti's benefit to lay hands on all my receipts in order to squeeze the guarantee money out of me."

Despite this contretemps, it seemed to the curious—and especially to Mapleson—that the Academy had conquered. Metropolitan directors were in despair. Unless they found a new manager quickly their house would remain dark the following season. But who was there left to try? Ernest Gye was again deemed a poor choice because it was feared he would favor his wife, the soprano Emma Albani, over Nilsson. Mapleson is reported to have made inquiries for the position but was also ruled out, probably because of his close identification with the enemy of the previous season.

## 4. *I cannot fight Wall Street*

So despondent were Metropolitan Opera directors after the 1883–84 season that they were willing to try anything during the 1884–85 season, even German opera. Just that was proposed in August 1884 by Leopold Damrosch, an energetic, bewhiskered fifty-two-year-old German-American conductor. He was available to salvage the biggest white elephant yet in American musical history, their opera house.

Damrosch was the conductor of both the recently organized New York Symphony Society and the New York Oratorio Society. In 1881 he had led a "monster" music festival at the Seventh Regiment Armory that lasted a week but took an entire winter to prepare. He was talkative, compulsive and would not delegate musical responsibilities to subordinates because he considered it "his solemn duty" to represent German art in the United States. He was much admired by local musicians for his artistic standards and much disliked by local musicians because a rehearsal sometimes lasted the entire day. At first glance an unlikely candidate for the Metropolitan position (he offered to present starless opera), Leopold Damrosch got the job because he promised costs would be held down and because Hillborn Roosevelt, president of his Symphony Society, recommended him to James Roosevelt, now president of the board of the Metropolitan.

Damrosch was clearly an economical sort. Metropolitan directors were happy to learn that his salary requirement was a modest $10,000 a year. Other good features were his offer to use his oratorio chorus, his symphony orchestra and low-fee Central European singers. Metropolitan directors asked only that Amalia Materna, who had appeared with great success at Theodore Thomas' music festival the year before, be included on the artists roster. Materna heard about the request, and on his subsequent recruiting drive in Europe Damrosch learned her fee was $1,000 per performance. The disconcerted impresario engaged her anyway, but in addition he obtained Marianne Brandt, Anton Schott and Marie Schröder-Hanfstängl, three amiable, tireless, magnificent, refreshingly low-paid artists.

While Damrosch was signing up German singers, Mapleson was searching Europe for Italian recruits. Despite victory the previous season, his situation was precarious. Patti remained on the payroll, but there was no refurbishing at the Academy, and the house was literally falling to pieces. During the 1884–85 season it would not be unusual for a patron's seat to buckle under him while he was enjoying an aria. The Academy was unsafe as well as unfashionable, and this combination even doughty Colonel Mapleson would not be able to overcome.

Mapleson led off the second season of competition on November 10, 1884, with a standard surefire spectacle—Patti in *Il Barbiere*. It was a promising success. A week later manager Damrosch entered the lists with *Tannhäuser*. His leads were unknown locally, conductor Damrosch was hardly flashy, but swarms of German-Americans attended, overwhelmed by the opportunity to applaud German art. The following evening Damrosch presented *Fidelio;* the only part of the house not filled to capacity was the stockholders' boxes. In a maddening reversal for Mapleson, interests of the New York music public had changed; throngs abandoned glamorous Italian opera for the ponderous mythology of Wagner.

In January, Metropolitan directors discovered that box-office receipts were running double the previous season's (though ticket prices had been lowered by half), and the chorus went on strike for a raise in pay. Damrosch refused to bargain with his choristers but agreed to reengage each at his previous salary if he apologized. Strike leaders were summarily fired. Keeping to the spirit of the economy drive, Damrosch agreed to a raise in salary of only $4,000 for the 1885–1886 season.

Working day and night at the Metropolitan in the service of German art, Damrosch continued rehearsing and leading Oratorio Society and Symphony Society concerts. Inevitably his health suffered. In mid-February, with less than a week left until the end of the season, he collapsed at a rehearsal. Four days later he died. The Metropolitan board allowed the house to be used for funeral services and voted for Damrosch's son Walter to complete the season and to fulfill tour engagements as Metropolitan conductor in Chicago, Cincinnati and Boston.

Over at the Academy, Mapleson continued to enjoy good health, but his fortunes had sunk to a new low. Patti was still on the roster, but a lack of solid male leads hurt badly, and the trickle of patrons to enemy ranks at the Met had risen to flood tide.

In November 1885, Mapleson began his last season at the Academy, ignored by remaining directors, deserted by Patti and explaining to the press that the star system was all wrong. He opened with Minnie Hauk in *Carmen;* public response was so poor that the entire season lasted twelve evening and four afternoon performances. The manager took his weary artists on tour, bettering his fortunes in Boston and Philadelphia but suffering losses in New Orleans and St. Louis. In December he was back at the Academy to present *Manon Lescaut* for his own benefit and to deliver the remark by which history best remembers him: "I cannot fight Wall Street." Mapleson gave a short season at the Metropolitan Opera House before he quit New York for Boston, where he slunk out of the harbor evading process servers who bore a summons from Patti, to whom he owed money.

Metropolitan directors were stunned by Damrosch's death, but the policy of presenting German opera (and Italian operas sung in German) was not changed. Walter Damrosch was judged too young for his father's position as managing director, and Anton Schott, a tenor who boosted himself for the job, too noisy and aggressive. Edmund C. Stanton, Executive Secretary of the Board, who once confessed that he "did not know one side of the stage from another or a wing from a fly," was judged the best man available.

Stanton was young, worth $3 million and related to another board member. He was tall and handsome, and he shook the scenery before performances to make sure that it would not collapse. Stanton's chief duties were to attend to business details of the German Grand Opera Company and to stay out of Anton Seidl's way. Seidl was the new artistic director, a conductor who had worked under Wagner in Bayreuth and led the way for Wagner opera in New York with first American performances of *Die Meistersinger, Tristan und Isolde, Siegfried, Götterdämmerung* and *Das Rheingold*.

From 1884 to 1891, Metropolitan directors were bored by the artistic fare but thankful that it was inexpensive. They were praised in the press as art patrons rendering a public service, but they chattered incessantly during performances. Their German artists continued to sing with a diligence unheard among Italian colleagues. Marianne Brandt sang three roles in twenty-four hours; Lilli Lehmann sang six Brunnhildes in eight days; and Josef Staudigl sang a Wotan one afternoon and a Leporello that evening.

Magnificent singing notwithstanding, by the 1890–91 season, Stanton's last as manager, the patience of directors with German opera was wearing thin. Conversation among boxholders grew so loud during performances that stockholders took to shushing each other. A notice posted in each box on January 15, 1891, decried "the annoyance produced by the talking in the boxes," and called for it to be discontinued "By order of the Board of Directors."

Stanton tried to hold down conversation during his final

season by varying the fare. He offered Baron Alberto Franchetti's *Asrael*, Smareglia's *Il Vassallo di Szigeth* and the Duke of Saxe-Coburg's *Diana von Solange*, three operas not heard since. They were not well received at their premieres. "Simply rubbish," "bewildering," "a sup of horrors," said the critics.

At this crucial moment in Metropolitan history, the directors decided to bring back Henry Abbey.

In the spring of 1890, Abbey had leased the Metropolitan for a month of Italian opera featuring Nordica and Patti. Their old magic wove its spell. Conversation ceased in the boxes. But when it was announced that Abbey would present a season of French and Italian opera during the 1891–92 season, conversation grew louder in the balcony. Seidl was cheered wildly. "The Germans, who comprise three-fourths of the present patronage of the Metropolitan, will seldom darken its doors next season," wrote Henderson of the *Times*. "Whether or not there is a public to take their places is the problem."

## 5. *Gaze on, my children*

Henry E. Abbey, a manager saddled with debts of $584,000 in the spring of 1884, made such effective use of his partner, Maurice Grau, that by 1890 the firm of Abbey, Schoeffel and Grau was acknowledged to be the foremost theatrical agency in the country. "Grau provided the successes, [and] Abbey provided the losses over which Schoeffel did the grumbling," said *Musical America* in 1898. "It was the absolute confidence the artists had in Grau that gave Abbey the basis on which he used to borrow the money to meet the losses." With the help of his hyperactive partner Grau, Abbey dispatched Josef Hofmann, Pablo de Sarasate, Adelina Patti, the Lillian Russell Opera Company, London's Gaiety Theatre Company, Ellen Terry and dozens of other musicians and thespians to large and to small cities, much in the manner of Napoleon Bonaparte dispatching the legions. The "little Napoleon," they called Abbey in the trade.

The return of the threesome to offices at the Metropolitan Opera House was marked by a gathering of stars whose aggregate talents were breathtaking and by a new agreement between stockholders and impresarios that was to endure for fifteen years. The talents included such legendary figures as Jean and Édouard de Reszke, Emma Eames, Nordica, Lehmann, Sembrich, Jean Lassalle and Patti (for nonsubscription performances). Within three seasons they were to be joined by Emma Calvé, Nellie Melba, Victor Maurel, Francesco Tamagno and Pol Plançon. According to the terms of agreement Abbey took the Metropolitan at an annual rental fee of $52,000 and pledged to present opera four times each week for thirteen weeks; Metropolitan stockholders paid $52,000 for box privileges and reserved the right to nominate six singers on the artists' roster, two of whom were to take part in each subscription performance.

On December 14, 1891, after performances in Chicago, Abbey's reborn Italian Grand Opera Company took to the Metropolitan stage for the first time. The opera was Gounod's *Roméo et Juliette*, the stars were Eames and the de Reszkes, and the impact of the singers was not immediately felt. Eames was called a "strikingly beautiful Juliette," Édouard de Reszke was hailed as "a really great artist," but Jean de Reszke's voice was said to be an "agreeable though not a surprising organ." In mid-January, when Grau cast the de Reszkes and Lassalle in *L'Africaine*, the virtues of the company were more apparent. "To see three such splendid representations of physical and artistic manhood . . . on the stage was in itself a unique sensation," said Henry Krehbiel of the *Tribune*. Evidently anxious to please all the customers during this season, the impresarios presented *Lohengrin, Fidelio* and *Die Meistersinger* (all in Italian) in addition to French and Italian works. Such large audiences turned out that Abbey felt called upon to bring his company back for an extra two weeks after the regular season.

This auspicious renascence for Abbey, Schoeffel and Grau came to an abrupt end when the interior of the supposedly fireproof Metropolitan was destroyed by fire in August 1892. The following season was canceled, and lukewarm Metropolitan stockholders took the opportunity to depart the fold. It was announced that the Metropolitan Opera-house Co., Ltd., would not rebuild the house, but nineteen faithful opera fans decided to try again and convinced sixteen other society figures to help buy the building from the old corporation and pay for reconstruction, despite the fact that only 25 percent of damage costs could be recovered from insurance. The indomitable thirty-five began to rebuild in April of 1893 for the 1893–94 season. Their corporation had a new name, the Metropolitan Opera and Real Estate Company, and a new system of support: each patron took $30,000 in stock and also purchased $30,000 in bonds to finance reconstruction. When the house was reopened it had 350 more orchestra seats (the ground-floor boxes had been removed), new scenery and new costumes.

Metropolitan audiences during the 1893–94 season saw a renewed emphasis on all-star casts. The opening-night work, *Faust*, was sung by the de Reszkes, Lassalle and Eames; *Carmen* was sung on December 20 by Calvé, Eames, Jean de Reszke and Lassalle. Alert to all possibilities, Abbey and Grau not only assembled "ideal casts" but toyed with the idea of producing *Il Barbiere* with an all-girl cast headed by Nellie Melba as the Count. This bauble was abandoned, but in answer to complaints about the quality of the chorus, they put the comeliest choristers in the front ranks. Previous and profitable experience presenting Lydia Thompson and her company of British blondes in *Faust-Up-to-Date* had taught them that a curvaceous singer could be every bit as valuable as an artistic one.

Tickets for Metropolitan extravaganzas were priced as high as $5 if "ideal casts" appeared. The following season, 1894–95, the top was raised to $7 when the de Reszkes, Plançon, Nordica, Scalchi, Melba and Maurel were all packed into a single production of Meyerbeer's *Les Huguenots*.

"It is not often that any opera house offers such an array of celebrities," wrote Henderson, critic for the *Times*, but he still found things to criticize. "The whole enterprise is devoted to the glorification of the leading artists." Henderson singled out Nellie Melba for a broadside. "[She] giggles, makes faces, nods to acquaintances in the opera club's boxes and generally comports herself in a free and untrammeled manner in the most serious scenes of her roles. Her occasional attempts at acting are ludicrous. But she is thoroughly satisfied with herself, and her public is thoroughly satisfied with her." Jean de Reszke called forth much the same public adoration—at one of his performances sixteen women are said to have fainted—but Henderson could see more virtue in his artistry: ". . . the greatest tenor of the 19th century; his retirement from the stage would practically mean the collapse of opera as at present given in New York."

To these brilliant, magnetic, dynamic, giggling stars, Abbey paid high fees. Jean de Reszke received $10,000 per month for eight performances plus 25 percent of receipts over $5,000. His brother Édouard received $600 per month plus 10 percent of receipts over $5,000. Melba was on a par with Jean de Reszke, except she did not receive a percentage. Eames earned $1,000 per night, and Calvé, whose Carmen was "a creature of unbridled passion," earned $1,500 per performance. What economies were practiced pertained to supporting artists. Choristers earned $15 per week, orchestra players earned $50 per week and the whole ballet shared $10,000 for an entire season's work.

In the 1895–96 season the managers launched "Nights of the Seven Stars" during which Nordica, Melba, Scalchi, the de Reszkes, Plançon and Maurel sang Meyerbeer's *Huguenots* for a $7 top. So successful were the "Nights" that they were repeated at matinées. Commenting on one such afternoon performance, the *Times* observed that "several people were carried out in a fainting condition." Indicatively, the evening performance of Verdi's *Falstaff* that followed "was given to

an audience which occupied less than one-half the auditorium"
—its cast included only two stars, Scalchi and Maurel.

A major tactical error made by Abbey and Grau was to deny
use of the Metropolitan Opera House to Walter Damrosch
for one of his jousts with German opera and thus to lose his
cooperation in obtaining German artists. The impresario-con-
ductor took his company to the Academy and presented
*Fidelio, Lohengrin,* the Ring operas, *Tannhäuser* and his own
*Scarlet Letter.* A loss of $43,000 dampened his enthusiasm,
but this was mitigated by news that Abbey had, with characteristic determination, taken losses of $150,000 on his Ger-
man opera productions the season before. Grau finally suggested an exchange of artists, the Metropolitan to get
Damrosch's Katharina Klafsky, whom it badly needed for
German works, and Damrosch to get Emma Calvé, whom he
badly needed for French and Italian works. The solution was
eminently acceptable to Damrosch, who was beginning to feel
that Wagner opera alone "was not sufficient to give a well-
balanced opera season. . . ."

With their Metropolitan Opera affairs in order and the
competition pacified, Abbey, Schoeffel and Grau settled back
peacefully into a series of disasters that wrecked their agency.

The troubles began when Abbey opened Abbey's Theatre
in New York, dispatched several artists on unsuccessful tours
and premiered Herman Bemberg's unsuccessful opera *Elaine*
at the Metropolitan. Abbey, Schoeffel and Grau overextended
themselves financially and went bankrupt. A settlement was
reached with creditors and William Steinway loaned the
struggling agency $50,000, but its days were numbered.

On October 17, 1896, Abbey died, and the following month
William Steinway passed away. Bereft of partner and angel,
Grau struggled vainly to assemble all-star casts. Even before
the season began he was desperate for a dramatic soprano.
Nordica was willing to sing for $1,100 per night in view of
Grau's difficulties but learned that Melba had settled for
$1,200 plus a percentage. Nordica decamped in a huff, the

final blow being a tip that Grau had promised Melba exclusive rights to the role of Brünnhilde. Katharina Klafsky, a soprano who might have solved some of Grau's German opera problems, died before the season began as the result of an operation for a head injury. Melba, out during the early part of the season preparing for Brünnhilde, did such a poor job in the role that she advised Grau, "It is beyond me. I have been a fool." She then despaired and asked for a release from her contract. This Grau was happy to give her, because it allowed him to cast Eames as Juliette in Gounod's *Roméo et Juliette*, a role hitherto reserved for Melba.

As if casting problems weren't enough, a series of midweek matinées Grau launched on November 21 was a box-office failure, Emma Eames fell ill, a projected *Le Nozze di Figaro* was dropped, a sixty-three-year-old baritone died on stage during a performance of *Martha*, the critics pounced on Grau for giving *Faust* for the tenth time that season ("The Faust-spielhaus," Henderson called the Metropolitan) and the novelty of the season, Massenet's *Le Cid*, was derided in the press "as a deadly piece of weariness."

The manager took to the road with his troupe in a vigorous effort to recoup his fortunes, opening in Chicago on February 22 with Calvé in *Carmen*. Five times the diva was put before Chicago music lovers in the same role, five times they applauded her wildly, and five times too few attended the performances. Even a reduction of tickets to "popular prices" —$2 in the orchestra and seventy-five cents in the balcony— failed to move customers into the house.

In his distress Grau was forced to borrow $30,000. Eleven thousand dollars came from the de Reszkes, Calvé and Lassalle, whose subsequent performances in St. Louis, Louisville, Cincinnati and Boston added little to the profit column. The tour was a financial catastrophe.

One day, weeks after the Chicago performances, while the troupe was wending its way back to New York, the discouraged impresario was looking out of a train window

disconsolately. An artist noticed him in his solitude and called
on the impresario to join a group also watching the blooming
spring countryside. "Gaze on, my children," he told them,
"and gaze long at this wondrous spectacle. It is the last time
that any of you will ever view it at my expense."

It was.


## 6. *Singers who draw big houses*

Maurice Grau seldom volunteered judgments, but his considered observations have a pungency unusual in the annals
of management. "Singers who draw big houses are worth big
money," he told an artist hoping for a raise. "I can't understand why you think you're one of them. No one has ever
demanded his money back because a performance of yours
was cancelled." Grau's four conductors at the Metropolitan
shared $20,000 in salaries annually. "No one ever paid a
nickel to see a man's back," said Grau, who never offered
*them* raises either. A scrupulous businessman, he always hon-
ored an agreement to the letter. "Maurice will give you a cigar,
but he would refuse to give you a match to light it with, if it
wasn't in the bargain," said Jean de Reszke.

At the peak of his career during the closing years of the
nineteenth century, Grau was a short, bearded, round-shoul-
dered manager who read the fine print in contracts carefully
and, if a clause was vague but could be interpreted to his
advantage, interpreted the vague clause to his advantage. He
had no artistic pretensions, boasted that he knew nothing
about music and said "the art lies in making money. . . ."
Grau disconcerted superstitious singers with his tuneless
whistling and avoided buying stage sets, costumes and other
nonproductive items. The commission Metropolitan stars paid
the opera house for the use of its name in advertisements for
concerts and recordings dates from his reign at the house.
(The practice was ended only after a long battle with the

American Guild of Musical Artists during the 1930s.) His major interests were his family, his work and poker, which he played whenever he had the opportunity. In the five years he managed a troupe at the Metropolitan, he accumulated a fortune estimated at $600,000 from salary, profits and stock-market transactions. He systematized procedures, presented the greatest singers of his time and demanded that society attend gala events in dress clothes.

The impresario did not immediately launch into plans to achieve these goals following the ill-fated 1896–97 season. Abbey's death, an absence of female stars in his troupe, and above all, a pressing need for time to think things out, militated against a quick return to activity. Grau presented a brief post-season of opera at the Metropolitan (which included a benefit for Kitty K. Abbey, Henry's daughter), announced that he had signed a three-year lease with directors and sublet to Walter Damrosch for presentations of German operas. A happy surprise after several months of disasters was news that he had been chosen to succeed Sir Augustus Harris at Covent Garden in London, largely through the recommendation of Jean de Reszke. Thanks to simultaneous management of the Metropolitan and Covent Garden, Grau established a world monopoly on singers and had his choice of the greatest talents available.

While Damrosch was busy at the Metropolitan, Grau occupied himself with the reorganization of the firm of Abbey, Schoeffel and Grau. Schoeffel was an early casualty in a grim attempt to achieve stability. "John Schoeffel was not much more than the hyphen between Abbey and Grau," said one observer, and Grau sold his stolid partner the only asset left to the old firm, the Tremont Theater in Boston, which Schoeffel retired northward to manage. Grau then offered creditors one-third on their statements, which they accepted, in return for a clean bill of financial health. Capital for a new agency was obtained through friends such as the Tysons, already important in New York as ticket brokers, and Henry

Dazian, the costumer. Grau neither applied to nor received money from the rich.

The "Grau Grand Opera Company" that appeared from 1897 to 1903 at the Metropolitan consisted of the brightest stars of earlier firmaments—Sembrich, Lehmann, Nordica, Eames, Plançon, the de Reszkes—and eventually included Ernestine Schumann-Heink, Anton Van Rooy, Ernest Van Dyck and David Bispham as well. Under Grau's management the Metropolitan passed from the era of "ideal casts" to the "Golden Age of Song." Superlatives are inadequate in an attempt to describe the vocal qualities of his singers. Grau's practice was to assemble the greatest cast possible and let it sing; the practice flowered in a *Tristan* with Nordica or Lehmann, the de Reszkes and Bispham or Van Rooy; a *Don Giovanni* with Lehmann, Sembrich, Nordica, Maurel and Édouard de Reszke; a *Tannhäuser* with Eames, Nordica, Van Dyck and Plançon. Among other novelties, the impresario presented the first unabridged cycle of Ring operas in New York, the Metropolitan's first (and thus far only) opera by a female composer (Ethel Smyth's *Der Wald*), Ignace Jan Paderewski's dreary *Manru*, and the most expensive premiere of his career, an opera by Louis Reyer entitled *Salammbô*. Puccini's *Tosca*, another of his premieres, entered the repertory over his protests. "An opera with a torture scene, a murder, a shooting and a suicide!" Grau cried to Emma Eames. "Not even you could make the public like it." The great entrepreneur was cajoled by Eames into presenting the work. Eventually other singers did make the public like it, but not before the *Times* called *Tosca* "repulsive" and Krehbiel said it was "hideous."

From morning to night, Grau sat before his large rolltop desk alternately adding singers to his roster as they proved successful and dropping singers from his roster as they failed to draw. Beginning in 1899, his troupe traversed the nation annually; during his first three touring years, it visited thirty-seven cities, twenty-three of them for the first time in Metropolitan history. Foot-high letters on trains proclaimed "The Metropolitan Opera House." This blatant legend offended many a dignified onlooker, but Grau believed in advertising his product whichever way possible. Alas, the desired effect was sometimes lost. On a tour in October 1901 a Rochester audience had the dubious honor of providing the lowest box-office figure yet in Metropolitan Opera history—$332.00.

Of more lasting value was Grau's attempt to develop a guarantee system that would build a national audience for the Metropolitan. In Kansas City a sponsor named S. Kronenberg agreed to pay him $12,500, regardless of how many people attended three Metropolitan performances. Kronenberg later gave guarantees for Metropolitan presentations in Lincoln, Minneapolis, Buffalo and Cleveland, allowing these cities to hear the same matchless performers New York heard. In Los Angeles, Grau exacted a guarantee of $14,000 from L. E. Behymer for a *Carmen* with Calvé, a *Lohengrin* with Sembrich, Schumann-Heink and Bispham, and a *Les Huguenots* with Johanna Gadski, Louise Homer, Antonio Scotti, Marcel Journet and Édouard de Reszke.

But by 1902, the manager was a somber dyspeptic whose health was breaking under the strain of constant worry and ceaseless travel. During summers Grau searched Europe for new talent; during winters he searched America for new places to present it. "Well, Grau is tired," he told a San Francisco newspaperman. "I shall quit while the luck is still hot, and the funeral of Maurice Grau will not be paid for by his friends."

In New York that season there were indications that the luck was growing cold. "What is there in our performances [of Gounod's *Roméo et Juliette*] but the imposing line-up of celebrities before the curtain at the end of the Garden scene?" asked Henderson of the *Times*. And, in truth, the impresario never offered much in the way of precise ensembles or sumptuous settings. He frowned on extra rehearsals—they cost extra money—and rationalized that the Metropolitan was no place for beginners. In Baltimore, his compulsive drive to cut costs led to a performance of *Lohengrin* with a boating scene on the Thames as a backdrop, this being the only setting handy. When two of his leading lights—Jean de Reszke and Melba—retired from the Metropolitan after the 1899–1900 season, Grau had precious little merchandise to offer. By 1902, it was time for the impresario to leave the Metropolitan too.

Grau's retirement was announced during the 1902–03 season. He recommended no successor and remained aloof from the fray during a bitter scramble for his position. The manager took a villa in Croissy-Chatou near Paris, but maintained a lively interest in the American musical scene. For several years rumors circulated in New York that he would return to undertake new theatrical assignments. Oscar Hammerstein, it was said, wanted him to head his Manhattan Opera House, which opened in 1907 and was intended to provide low-cost opera for the masses. Grau lent credence to this report by telling a correspondent that management should develop mass interest in opera rather than cater to the wishes of "society."

Grau did not live to see any plans mature for his reentry on the American scene. Suffering from Bright's disease, he passed away in 1907. His death called forth tributes to his promotional abilities from friends, colleagues and artists. The Metropolitan Opera House staff recalled his sincerity and fairness, the newspapers his "ideal casts." A saddened Nellie Melba said that "Grand opera in the United States could not have been what it is now had it not been for him." And true to his own prediction, his funeral was not paid for by his friends.

# PART TWO
## *Patrons*

Lorenzo Da Ponte, organizer and co-manager of the first opera house in New York City. *(Museum of the City of New York)*

Italian Opera House, New York. It opened on November 18, 1833, at the corner of Leonard and Church streets. *(Museum of the City of New York)*

Jenny Lind (*Museum of the City of New York*)

"Jenny Lind and the Americans—Coronation of Jenny the First—
Queen of the Americans." Cartoon from *Punch,* October 5, 1850.
*(Museum of the City of New York)*

New York Academy of Music in 1854, when it opened. Photo from
cover of souvenir book on the occasion of the closing of the Academy
of Music in 1926. *(Museum of the City of New York)*

William Steinway *(John Steinway)*

Maurice Grau *(Museum of the City of New York)*

Colonel Mapleson (*Culver Pictures, Inc.*)

Henry Lee Higginson *(Boston Symphony Orchestra)*

Otto H. Kahn (High Fidelity/Musical America)

Oscar Hammerstein I, 1908 *(Museum of the City of New York)*

Left to right, L. E. Behymer and Sol Hurok (High Fidelity/Musical America)

John D. Rockefeller III, chairman of the board of directors, Lincoln Center for the Performing Arts. *(Lincoln Center for the Performing Arts. Photograph by Arnold Newman)*

Left to right, John D. Rockefeller III, President Eisenhower, David M. Keiser, Robert Moses, Manhattan Borough President Hulan Jack, New York Mayor Robert F. Wagner, and New York Lieutenant Governor Malcolm Wilson at ground-breaking ceremonies for Lincoln Center for the Performing Arts. *(Lincoln Center for the Performing Arts. Photograph by Bob Serating)*

# V. *The Aristocrat of Orchestras*

*"Musicians are not like other men, and must be treated differently; but patience, discipline, and tact fetch good results."*

—Major Henry L. Higginson

## 1. *There has sprung up a desire*

"The americans are certainly a music-loving people," Theodore Thomas, America's leading orchestral conductor, wrote by way of introduction to an article in the March 1881 issue of *Scribner's Magazine*. "They are peculiarly susceptible to the sensuous charm of tone, they are enthusiastic and learn easily, and with the growth in general culture of recent years, there has sprung up a desire for something serious in its purpose in music, as in the other arts."

Thomas entitled his article "Musical Possibilities in America," but could cite few real opportunities for professional instrumentalists. New York, he reported, was the one city in the nation where an orchestral player could earn a living, and here only by supplementing his income giving lessons and playing at balls. Boston could not support a "large well-balanced orchestra." In Cincinnati and Chicago orchestral musicians were eking out their livings playing in beer gardens and in saloons. There was a demand only for "piano players," and then mainly as teachers.

"I think it is in the vocal direction, and not in the instrumental, that the present development of the art tends," Thomas thought gloomily. "Singing . . . appeals to almost every one, and there is a certain demand, even if limited, for singers in the churches." Like opera, choral festivals were popular, audiences enjoying the spectacles of mammoth (and nonprofessional) choruses as much as the compositions performed. Opera and oratorio were infinitely more pleasing than instrumental music, which was "mysterious" and "learned." The multitudes could make nothing of music without text or plot, of abstract tonal experiences labeled symphonies, overtures and concertos.

Further proof of lack of interest in the symphonic literature was that the United States did not possess a single orchestra equal to one of the great European ensembles. The New York Philharmonic, organized in 1842, gave only six concerts and six public rehearsals per season in rented quarters. Efforts to raise money for a hall of its own had failed. Its conductors were elected by its members, and its members felt no qualms about sending in substitutes on concert nights, should more lucrative engagements be available. This made for a characteristic insecurity at performances, elected conductors never being entirely certain which musicians they would face. Artistic successes were rare; the discipline to produce them was almost nonexistent.

The Philharmonic's finances were as shaky as its artistry. It was organized on a cooperative basis and its members shared in profit and loss. The cost of operations was met by ticket sales, by membership dues from musicians and by fines levied on absentees. Earnings were never high. Dividends per artist per season dropped to a low of $17.50 in 1878 and were to reach a high of only $225 in 1886. Professional musicians regarded the orchestra as an opportunity to earn some extra money, not as a serious professional enterprise.

Happily, the behavior of audiences had improved over the years. In its early days the Philharmonic played to loud, rude and boisterous music lovers—"the ebulliency of animal spirits sometimes overcame their sense of decorum"—but in 1867 a non-playing associate member, Dr. R. Ogden Doremus of New York University, was elected president and promptly began a campaign to improve the orchestra's standing. Doremus, a chemistry professor, insisted that it be increased to one hundred men and that prominent soloists be engaged. Thanks to the size of the ensemble and glamorous names, Philharmonic concerts became important social events, especially attractive to those whose religious beliefs prevented them from going to the opera or to the theater.

It was dismay at Philharmonic performances that led Thomas, a Philharmonic violinist, to organize his own orchestra in 1862 when he was twenty-eight. In 1868 he conducted it in the first of the famous summer concerts in Central Park Garden, an auditorium in Central Park surrounded by open spaces filled with tables at which light refreshments were served. Between May 1868 and October 1875 Thomas and his orchestra gave 1,127 concerts in the Garden, more concerts than the Philharmonic had given during its entire history. Thomas served not only as music director and conductor but as manager and fund raiser, too.

In its quality and in the scope of its repertory, the Thomas Orchestra was a revelation for musicians and audiences. It performed every evening nearly half the year; Thomas paid his men high salaries and engaged the finest orchestral players in the nation. The orchestra rehearsed daily, reaching an unparalleled level of technical competence. Stable personnel made possible artistic discipline, unknown at the Philharmonic. Though the Thomas Orchestra numbered only forty players at its inception, it was increased to fifty and then to sixty thoroughly drilled performers.

Thomas also worked hard to increase and to interest audiences. His programs included light works that did not strain the capacities of untrained listeners but sent them home whistling tunes. When interest appeared to be rising, Thomas programmed complete symphonies. Audiences as well as musicians became familiar with a large part of the orchestral literature and heard works by Wagner, Liszt, Tchaikovsky and other contemporary masters for the first time.

In 1869 Thomas took his musicians on the first of nine annual tours of the East and the Middle West. He served as a musical pioneer, laying the groundwork for great orchestras to follow but enduring unwarranted criticism from "critics" who claimed that he programmed too much "classical" music. Never would he lower his standards. Anton Rubinstein, who performed with Thomas in New York and on tour, wrote William Steinway that "Never in my life . . . have I found an orchestra that was as perfect as the organization Theodore Thomas has created and built up."

But in 1877 Thomas was elected conductor of the New York Philharmonic and went over to the camp of the enemy; he explained that it was "better for the cause of art that a society rather than an individual should be in authority." What he meant was that he was tired of carrying the financial burden of the Thomas Orchestra himself. The orchestra was an artistic success, but not a financial one. Thomas was tired of hectic schedules, of having to devise ways to perform more concerts, of traveling constantly to earn enough to pay his men.

"We want an end of amateurism in teachers and other professionals," Thomas pleaded in his *Scribner's* article. "We need some provision for the talent which is developing every day—we need [an] institution, well endowed, which will not be obliged to adopt a mere commercial standard for want of the means of support." He had shown the way to high standards of orchestral performance. His example of lofty idealism had inspired musicians throughout the nation. But where were the musical philanthropists, Esterhazys of the New World, to ease his way?

## 2. *Almost my inner world*

The same month that readers pondered Thomas' words, Major H. L. Higginson, a Boston financier, placed an announcement in local newspapers:

THE BOSTON SYMPHONY ORCHESTRA
IN THE INTEREST OF GOOD MUSIC

Notwithstanding the development of musical taste in Boston, we have never yet possessed a full and permanent orchestra, offering the best music at low prices, such as may be found in all the large European cities, or even in the smaller musical centres of Germany. The essential condition of such orchestras is their stability, whereas ours are necessarily shifting and uncertain, because we are dependent upon musicians whose work and time are largely pledged elsewhere.

To obviate this difficulty the following plan is offered. It is an effort made simply in the interest of good music. . . .

Before offering his plan, Major Higginson paused to praise the "previously existing musical organizations" that brought culture to Boston. He than launched into details:

The orchestra is to number sixty selected musicians. . . .
Mr. Georg Henschel will be the conductor. . . .
The concerts will be twenty in number. . . .

The price of season tickets, with reserved seats, for the whole series of evening concerts will be either $10 or $5, according to position.

Single tickets, with reserved seats, will be seventy-five cents or twenty-five cents, according to position.

Besides the concerts, there will be a public rehearsal on one afternoon of every week, with single tickets at twenty-five cents, and no reserved seats.

Higginson ended with hopes that:

This orchestra shall be made permanent here, and shall be called the "Boston Symphony Orchestra."

Both as the condition and result of success the sympathy of the public is asked.

Plan, announcement, and a decision to give concerts on Saturday nights—heretofore almost barren of entertainments in Boston—were the sole doing of the Major, at forty-six reportedly worth $750,000 and a member of the family firm of Lee, Higginson and Company.

Major Higginson was a descendant of sturdy Puritan pioneers. He was energetic, strong-willed, hard-working, straightforward, trusted by his business associates, but known more for "steadiness of character" than for "extraordinary mentality." Higginson is said to have been an easy mark for confidence men, and had had a somewhat checkered career, being in turns a student at Harvard (he did not graduate), a clerk, a wine merchant, a worker in the Ohio oil fields, and manager of a Georgia cotton plantation that went bankrupt. He had also traveled in Europe, studied music in Vienna, and served in the Army of the Potomac during the Civil War, from whence came the title "Major."

The struggle had a profound effect on Higginson, an abolitionist who considered duty an imperative. "That war taught a great many men that if we were to have a country worthy of the name, we must work for it, educate it, as well as fight for it . . . ," he wrote in *An Account of the Boston Symphony Orchestra* in 1911. "Such had been the creed of the men with whom I had lived from boyhood, and as most of them were killed in the war, my duty was the greater in order to fill up the gap which their death [sic] had left." Higginson was commissioned a second lieutenant, was severely wounded in his first engagement (he bore a saber scar across his face for the rest of his life), and was discharged a major.

Music, like duty, was another imperative. "[Music] is almost my inner world," he wrote his father from Vienna in September 1857. "Without it, I miss much, and with it I am happier and better." Young Higginson dreamed of a career as a pianist, a dream that was shattered by an arm injury. A career as a composer was ruled out by instructors who found him studious but unoriginal. "[Writing music] is like writing poetry," he advised his father. "If one is prompted to do so, and has anything to say, he does it. But I entirely disavow any such intention." Higginson continued, "I am studying for my own good and pleasure," and returned to Boston undecided about his future but certain that music would be an avocation.

Higginson's studies in Vienna were to be crucial in the development of the Boston Symphony Orchestra. He came to the belief—never shaken—that Viennese musicians were the best in the world. Whenever in need of musical counsel he was to travel back to Vienna to consult with trusted advisers. In essence, a Massachusetts version of Viennese orchestras was to be created.

Though he could not vie with professional musicians as virtuoso or as composer, Higginson felt perfectly competent to choose the musical fare of Boston, mostly as a public service. As early as 1873 he was ready to embark on plans for an ensemble of European excellence, but was deterred by a business panic. Eight years later, still convinced of the rightness of his idea, he wrote that Boston needed an orchestra to give "as many serious concerts of classical music as [are] wanted, and also to give at other times, and more especially in the summer, concerts of a lighter kind of music . . . to do the same in neighboring towns and cities as far as is practicable, but certainly to give Harvard University all that she needs in this line. . . ."

Anything worthy could be put on programs, which were to be relatively brief, an hour and three quarters being the upper limit. "Anything unworthy" (defined as the "trash . . . heard in the theatres, sentimental or sensational nonsense. . . .") was to be kept off programs. Wagner could be played but was not among the Major's favorites. Late Beethoven, possibly "the work of a lunatic," might also be heard, since as a fair-minded

Yankee, Higginson could not see barring "serious music." "In short," he concluded, "all the catholicity possible seems to me good," and included among his own choices overtures to operas by Méhul, Boieldieu, Auber and Grétry.

Higginson grew more adventurous when considering the orchestra's financing, incorporating in his plan elements of capitalistic enterprise absent in Vienna, where musical organizations got subsidies. He estimated the total cost per season of an orchestra with sixty players would be $100,000. One half, or $50,000, could be recovered in ticket revenues. The other half Higginson himself resolved to provide; this would necessitate the investment "of $1,000,000 in principal." In addition, he would sell the orchestra's services to opera companies, though never at less than a "fair market price." An economical sort, he decided against offering pensions to musicians, thinking it best that "each musician should lay aside yearly something and thus pension himself."

Despite this steely attitude the Major was to offer to musicians what no other American philanthropist had yet offered them: guaranteed employment on a contractual, annual basis. They would be his full-time employees. In turn, he would sell their collective services to the public and subsidize the inevitable deficits. No better plan had yet been proposed in America. And for thirty-seven years it would be followed with only slight deviations.


### 3. *In numerical order*

Boston, a city in which aristocrats leaned over backward to display unostentatious good taste, had only 363,000 inhabitants in 1881, and was given to setting musical precedents. In 1728 it heard the first public concert in the Colonies; in 1730 it heard the second public concert, which was presented by Peter Pelham, a portrait painter and the stepfather of John Singleton Copley. Boston teemed with amateur choruses, and in 1823 its Handel and Haydn Society pressed a commission for an oratorio on Beethoven, who entered the request in a notebook but never acted on it. It was also in Boston that John Sullivan Dwight published his *Journal of Music*, the most influential music periodical in the nation.

Bostonians generally favored choral music over instrumental music. The city had nonetheless seen several attempts to found orchestras. The earliest was in 1810 or 1811, when Johann Christian Gottlieb Graupner, who played oboe under Joseph Haydn's direction in London, organized the Philoharmonic, the first serious orchestra in America. A Musical Fund Orchestra and a Philharmonic Orchestra followed. Between 1848 and 1854 the Germania Orchestra, an ensemble composed of German immigrants, made its headquarters in Boston. The Germanians toured the nation playing concerts, providing accompaniments for vocal soloists, and giving *Gesangvereine* orchestral support.

Despite all these orchestras, the citizenry never troubled to build a concert hall. When Jenny Lind arrived in Boston in 1851 there was no auditorium available, and the soprano sang an uncomfortable concert in the Fitchburg Railroad Station. Nor could some Bostonians quite grasp the meaning of the term "professional orchestra." It was hard to understand why instrumentalists should not be willing to donate services, like the members of volunteer choruses.

The Harvard Musical Association, founded in 1837, sponsored orchestral concerts beginning in 1866. These events paved the way for Higginson's effort with programs intended for "persons of taste and culture" who liked "pure programmes above all need of catering to low tastes." The concerts also enjoyed the active support of Dwight, who claimed that the association's presentations were of a higher caliber than they were likely to be "in the hands of those who give concerts only to make money."

On the other hand, the quality of performers was low. Comparison with the Thomas Orchestra, ostensibly in the hands of those anxious to earn money, indicated that commerce had its virtues. The superiority of the New York group, demonstrated at Boston concerts year after year from 1869, was manifest: Bostonians paid Thomas the supreme compliment of imitation, modeling efforts after his. It is said that the energy of this fillip was soon dissipated, however, and affairs reverted to a low ebb.

It was at the last concert of the Harvard Musical Association's sixteenth season, in March 1881, that Higginson heard Georg Henschel, a bearded, thirty-one-year-old German baritone, composer and teacher, lead a performance of his own *Concert Overture*. Mightily impressed by the conductor's energy and youthful enthusiasm, Higginson invited him to form the BSO, as it came to be known, at an annual salary of ten thousand dollars. A one-year contract was duly signed, Higginson approving fully of Henschel's repertory, which would include "every one of the nine Beethoven symphonies, of course in numerical order."

Higginson's initial choice for music director was to be ill-fated. The demanding task of training a new orchestra was well beyond the abilities of a conductor yet to perform successfully with an old one. Henschel tried manfully to establish his authority with personnel—musicians were warned to pay attention during rehearsals—but his inexperience was painfully evident in ragged performances and ill-conceived tempi. "Not that we object to fire," a critic objected, "but we would rather be warmed by it than roasted in a furious conflagration."

Nor were all of Henschel's musicians first-rate performers. The conductor allowed regional loyalties to figure in his choices of players, and it was an easygoing band of Bostonians (musically speaking) that appeared at Boston Music Hall on Saturday nights for fees per man of six dollars per concert and three dollars per rehearsal.

The Major was not one to make a mistake twice, and when Henschel left Boston in 1884, he was replaced by Wilhelm Gericke, an experienced Viennese drillmaster who followed

Johannes Brahms as conductor of the "Gesellschaftsconcerte" and was also a conductor at the court opera. It was feared in the Boston press that Gericke had arrived too late. "I believe that a large number attended the symphony concerts . . . simply because they were fashionable," wrote Louis Elson of the *Advertiser*. "Poor Mr. Gericke! He comes from Vienna just in time to take charge of an enterprise in which public interest is waning, and lucky Mr. Henschel, he will leave it in a manner which will enable him to say that it only prospered when under *his* direction."

Poor Mr. Gericke was to have other problems too. For one thing, he became homesick. For another, his musicians complained about his verbose lectures in German and about his insistence on promptness at dull rehearsals, which began every morning at 9:30. "Non-arrival of steam or horse cars" did not excuse lateness at rehearsals, Gericke told guilty wretches. Worse, he dismissed players without compunction, importing Central European replacements with Higginson's approval. Because the BSO was neither unionized nor a cooperative like the New York Philharmonic, there was nothing personnel could do.

At first Gericke was also unpopular with audiences. His programs featured a strict classical diet leavened only with unfamiliar modern works by Brahms, Bruckner and Richard Strauss. The battle for acceptance by the public was finally won by superb demonstrations of orchestral finesse and precision at home and in New York, still arbiter of the nation's music despite its lack of ensembles. After the BSO's Steinway Hall debut in February 1887, *The New York Times* found it had a "splendid masculinity" and that Gericke "placed himself and his musicians squarely on their merits before this public trusting nothing to the riot of revolution, but everything to serenity of sound scholarship." A performance of Handel's *Largo* by eighteen violinists strung out across the front of the stage smacked of mere showmanship but "under Gericke's direction, it was a surpassingly powerful interpretation and moved the audience as no orchestral playing has moved people in this city of recent years."

Two years later, Gericke was tired of struggling with non-German audiences and departed for Europe "amid floral tributes and gyrations of hats and handkerchiefs." To replace him, Higginson engaged the fiery, thirty-four-year-old Arthur Nikisch, the first of the "prima donna" conductors, a sartorial dandy whose elegance did not preclude an extraordinary personal magnetism and the ability to lead works from memory. It is said that "at his best, he was simply glorious," but at his worst Nikisch indulged in musical whimsies and forsook that orchestral precision and discipline so painfully developed by Gericke. His "undue passion in comparatively passionless melody" was decried, but never did Nikisch read reviews to find out why the commotion. For four seasons Boston was divided between those who admired Nikisch wildly and those who condemned the musical extravagances that led to a deterioration of orchestral finesse. The conductor quit the city in 1893, before his five-year contract had expired. Fanatical admirers were left sunk in despair, claiming that he had been driven from them by reactionary critics.

In succession, Higginson tried to reengage Gericke, who refused the bid, negotiated with Theodore Thomas, who was committed to the new Chicago Symphony Orchestra, and engaged Hans Richter, Wagner's favorite conductor at Bayreuth. Richter signed a contract for Boston, notwithstanding the fact that he had already signed a contract to conduct in Vienna during the same period. Faced with the Emperor Franz Joseph's displeasure, Richter opted to remain in Europe, and the Boston position went to Emil Paur, an Austro-Hungarian conductor who Higginson believed "had his own way of producing music."

Paur began well enough, but musicians and audiences found him dull after Nikisch. Every season there was a rumor that he would not return the next. Finally, in 1898, Paur went to New York and to the Philharmonic. Gericke was reengaged for a second rebuilding assignment and returned for eight more seasons.

It was found that the stern disciplinarian had not mellowed during the intervening years. The press said that he "repressed the instruments." As the years went by audiences drifted away. A suggestion by Higginson that Gericke invite guest conductors to appear—so that audiences might be increased—was refused testily. When he offered to leave a second time, after a total of thirteen seasons, Higginson was probably relieved to see him go.

In 1906, with a devotion unequalled in the history of American music, Higginson set about recruiting a replacement. Ideally he would obtain a Germanic conductor who was a combination of fire and precision, a quintessence of the BSO's four music directors.

## 4. *Steady, intelligent work*

The BSO was twenty-five years old in 1906 and had been brought back to such a state of efficiency by Gericke that it easily ranked as the nation's leading ensemble. It had served as model for "permanent" orchestras in three other cities, Chicago, Cincinnati and Pittsburgh. Its superiority over its predecessor, the New York Philharmonic, was unquestioned. The Philharmonic still gave only eight concerts per season and remained a cooperative, a "good thing" for superannuated members whose performances left much to be desired. Invidious comparisons between ensembles were made each season in New York; Gericke's initial concerts at Steinway Hall had developed into annual BSO series attended by large and enthusiastic crowds.

Major Higginson, seventy-one and gouty, was famous for his orchestra, renowned for his philanthropy and solicited for his donations. His gift list grew to include Princeton, Williams, the University of Virginia and Harvard, to which he gave $150,000 in 1899. He was a treasurer of Radcliffe and a fellow of the Harvard Corporation, for which he thwarted a plan to elect Theodore Roosevelt president of the university in 1909. The BSO remained his chief interest, "his racing stable, his library, and his art gallery," according to the philanthropist himself, who preferred to be its sole underwriter.

Higginson gladly shared his views on orchestral matters with the world, commenting that the development of a great ensemble was not much different from any other activity. "The success of the Orchestra has come from the same reason that brings success in any direction—steady, intelligent work in one line, and by faithful, intelligent men." Even intelligence might not be really important. "Anyone can do such a work who really tries," he reported.

Platitudes flowed easily from his pen. "Do we wonder at or praise a man who beautifies his own home, or makes happy his own household, by the free use of his thought, his time, or his money?" he asked rhetorically in a speech at the New York Harvard Club. "This beautiful land is our workshop, our playground, our garden, our home," he answered in a speech at the Chicago Harvard Club. "We can have no more urgent or pleasant task than to keep our workshop busy and content, our playground bright and gay, our garden well tilled and full of flowers and fruits, our home happy and pure." "Never mind the balance-sheet. Charge the deficit, if there be any, to profit and forget the loss, for it does not really exist," he urged listeners in a plea for art.

Higginson's success could not be faulted. A magnificent musical instrument had been created. Because of the achievement, even his platitudes could be forgiven. "Goodness gracious!" cried one observer after the earliest season, "How the symphony has become the very breath of our nostrils! And this after symphonies have been played for years to a few handfuls of aesthetic Boston ladies of either sex in the self-same hall, with about the same performers!" The improvements could be noted from year to year. During its first season, total attendance at performances was 83,359; during its second, attendance went up by a third to 111,777. As early as 1886 the orchestra earned $100,000 in five days of advance sales for twenty-four concerts and twenty-four public rehearsals of the "severest classical music." By 1888 the twenty concerts and the twenty public rehearsals of the first season had been increased to 112 performances.

Though more and more Bostonians clamored for seats, the Major tried to hold the line on ticket prices. Season rates of $10 and $5 "according to position" were maintained until the third season, when they went up to $12 and $6 respectively. In the twenty-sixth season, 1907–08, they were still only $18 and $10. The Major resorted to a Barnum-like solution in 1883 to prevent the resale of tickets at "advanced prices." He announced that "The prices of seats will remain as before, but a portion of the seats on the floor of the hall and in the first balcony will be disposed of for this season, at auction." A tradition was begun, bids going as high as $100, $150 and even $380 for one seat. The auction also brought on fear that less affluent music lovers would be priced out of the hall; it remained possible, however, to purchase seats for public rehearsals for as little as twenty-five cents.

Higginson himself continued to pay the highest price for attendance. Up to June 1893 he is known to have contributed $250,000 to meet deficits. It was, moreover, his example—and his threats—that inspired contributions for Symphony Hall, a permanent home for the BSO made necessary by the announced demolition of Music Hall in 1893. The Major said Symphony Hall would have to be ready for concerts in October 1894 (for the opening of the fourteenth season) or he would disband the orchestra. But he, Gericke, and the members of the ensemble were all on hand when the building was formally opened in October 1900.

As always, the Major kept a tight control over personnel. "I see no need or use for a Union," he wrote. "We pay more, ask entire control of the men and see to it that they are well paid. . . . On no other terms can I go on and pay a large subsidy and not control all this for the sake of art." Higginson nonetheless allowed the establishment of a Boston Symphony Orchestra Pension Institution in 1903, its funds derived from membership dues and from special Pension Fund concerts. The precedent was an important one. During the next half-century every major orchestra in the nation would thus provide for its retired musicians. A beginning was made to solving the problem of how musicians could be supported when they were too old to perform.

"The reason why the Boston Orchestra plays better than all other existing orchestras is—besides the excellent qualities of the men—the comfortable living the men are able to enjoy," explained Emil Paur, several years after his residency. "They all are paid better than anywhere else, consequently they have no sorrow of provisions; they feel free, satisfied, happy, not overworked, and the result is joy, enthusiasm, and perfection in their work." The maestro went on to explain why Boston audiences were enthusiastic: "The people nowadays fill the concerts of the Symphony Orchestra, not on account of the soloist, but only on account of the masterful playing of great musical works. The people in Boston know what they have, and love and appreciate gratefully the ideal thing which Major Higginson has nobly given them. The wonderful institution means an everlasting monument to the unselfish founder. . . ."

## 5. *A passion for perfection*

Higginson turned to the task of seeking conductor number five amid rumors that Nikisch would return to Boston. The new music director announced in June 1906, however, was Karl Muck, who had conducted orchestras in Berlin, Paris, Rome, St. Petersburg, London and Bayreuth, where he led performances of *Parsifal* in 1901. Higginson was undoubtedly impressed by the fact that Muck was also one of the regular conductors of the Vienna Philharmonic, the *ne plus ultra* of the world's ensembles.

Tall, spare, ascetic and aristocratic, Muck had none of the personal magnetism of Nikisch. As a youth he had pursued studies in classical philology, and his performances reflected a concern with discipline and exactness rather than with passion. Muck looked like a scholar and conducted like one— an unlikely combination to inspire orchestras and audiences. Yet his interpretations were deeply moving; an impeccable taste joined with a profound knowledge of the orchestral literature informed his readings. Moreover, he impressed his players at once with his humility. At his Boston debut, Muck put down his baton and allowed them to continue leaderless in a Beethoven symphony, thus publicly demonstrating confidence and respect for their abilities.

Muck's New York debut confirmed a general belief that Higginson had indeed found a conductor with qualifications to continue the "passion for perfection" that marked BSO performances. "The least of his concern is, to all appearances, the audience behind him . . . ," wrote Richard Aldrich of the *Times*. "He is clearly a man of authority and intellectual force, and he has that classical merit in a conductor of knowing what he wants and getting it." There was "a feeling," concluded Aldrich, that "Mr. Higginson had intrusted his men to safe hands."

Muck remained in Boston for two seasons, returning to Berlin in 1908 as general music director of the Berlin Opera. He was replaced by Max Fiedler, who was in turn replaced by Muck in 1912. This time Muck remained for six seasons, leading the ensemble to ever greater heights and causing Philip Hale of the *Boston Herald* to doubt it "possible to think of this orchestra without the vision of Dr. Muck at its head as the interpreter of beauty and brilliance. Fortunate, thrice fortunate, is he in having at his command this orchestra, largely his own creation; wholly the superb interpreter of composers as he understands them, as he shares in their emotions, confessions, declarations, griefs, and longings."

Indeed, Muck was almost the perfect choice. But it was

possible to think of the orchestra without the vision, and in 1918 he was the centerpiece of a scandal that ruined his American career and almost wrecked the BSO. A student of the case is at once struck by the poor judgment of almost everyone concerned.

The scandal had its origin in wartime hysteria. The United States declared war on Germany in April 1917 after a seesaw battle by Allied and German propagandists for the sympathy of the American people. The large German-American population was loyal, but there was fear of pro-German sentiments erupting into disloyal acts. A powerful, if unofficial, drive was begun to keep works by German composers off concert programs. Among outstanding examples, the New York City Board of Education ruled that German opera should not, as a product of "enemy" genius, be discussed at lectures. The directors of the New York Philharmonic, more liberal, prohibited only the performance of music by "living" Germans.

Muck, a German nationalist and friend of Wilhelm II, came under suspicion as an enemy agent. It was rumored that the conductor was plotting to kidnap millionaires living at Bar Harbor and to hold them for ransom; other demented patriots said that he had been overheard planning the dynamiting of both Faneuil Hall and the birthplace of Henry Wadsworth Longfellow.

The conductor was blissfully unaware of these ludicrous suspicions and went on leading the BSO with meticulous attention to musical detail. Meanwhile "citizens'" groups muttered that the BSO should not be permitted to perform in their communities unless its conductor was willing to begin concerts with "The Star Spangled Banner." Colonel Theodore Roosevelt went further and said that Muck should be locked up if he declined. Muck did not think much of the anthem but was willing to comply with the request and, as a matter of fact, did so in Boston and in New York. He neglected to do so in Providence, and the omission was later reported in the press in a manner that embarrassed both Muck and Higginson.

The conductor offered his resignation, which Higginson

declined to accept. A few days later Higginson told a BSO audience that "if the public wants to throw stones, let them throw them at me, not at the orchestra or the leader." He further inflamed patriots by a declaration that "art is a thing by itself and not related to any particular nation or group," and threatened to disband the orchestra. At eighty-two he was an angry albeit intensely pro-Allied patriot unable to fully comprehend the depth of wartime passions.

In late March 1918, Muck was suddenly and inexplicably arrested and taken to Fort Oglethorpe, where he remained until 1919, when he was sent back to Germany. No charges brought against him were ever made public. For the balance of the 1918–19 season a member of the orchestra acted as conductor.

Higginson's lifework began to crumble around him. There was now every indication that the anti-Germanism that had caused the debacle would stretch into the postwar era. Furthermore a Viennese or German musician and conductor would be *persona non grata*. The Major had personally expended $1 million on behalf of the BSO and now had neither strength nor funds to give. A month before Muck was seized, Higginson confided to a friend that "the burden" had become "almost intolerable." After considerable soul-searching, he retired in April. With him into retirement went the orchestra's manager, Charles A. Ellis. Bereft of sponsor, manager and conductor, the orchestra's ability to survive seemed doubtful. Paur's belief that "the people in Boston know what they have" was about to be put to a test.

Nine prominent Bostonians, among them some of the Major's closest friends, rose to the occasion and announced that they would apply to the state government for incorporation of the BSO. "It remains to be seen whether nine trustees will make a Major Higginson," said one, and it developed that nine trustees could. But without the financial help of Ernest B. Dane, who temporarily assumed Higginson's mantle, the orchestra would have verged on disaster.

Besides fund raising, Higginson's immediate successors faced the immediate problem of choosing a conductor. Owing to recent experience, German and Viennese aspirants were deemed unsuitable and offers were made to leaders of other nationalities. One celebrity after another declined (among them Arturo Toscanini and Sergei Rachmaninoff) for a variety of reasons, until Henri Rabaud, a Parisian, cabled his acceptance.

Though no longer at the helm, Higginson took a lively and critical interest in proceedings. "Rabaud, an admirable French conductor, is at the head, and the work should go on well," he wrote Gericke, still alive in Vienna. "But I often long for a concert such as you gave us—Haydn, Mozart, Beethoven, Schubert. Only a *Wiener Kind* can play Schubert." Less than a year later Higginson was dead, four days short of his eighty-fifth birthday.

In deference to the spirit in which he founded the orchestra, the trustees continued Higginson's anti-union policy. This led to a bitter strike in 1920. The issue was salary increases, but underlying all discussions was the problem of unionization. Trustees claimed that "as custodians of the orchestra rather than its financial sustainers they had no immediate means of increasing the income so as to raise the amount required." Thirty men promptly applied for union membership. The upshot was that the concertmaster and one third of the orchestra's personnel were dismissed.

Trustees congratulated each other that rebellion was crushed, but victory did not lead to permanent stability. Two decades later the BSO management was again forced to take the field against union organizers. The American Federation of Musicians threatened to boycott the orchestra's broadcasts and recordings, to prevent guest conductors and soloists from appearing with it and to blacklist concert halls in which the orchestra appeared while on tour. This time the forces arrayed against management were too strong. The only major non-unionized orchestra in the nation came to terms with the AFM in 1942.

It was indeed a mixed bag that the Major bequeathed. He set precedent for the support of orchestras, and despite his anti-union prejudice, the salaries of professional musicians throughout the country rose continually and were met for the next half-century by wealthy men upholding the philosophy of paternal capitalism that Higginson espoused. Charles Phelps Taft in Cincinnati, Charles Norman Fay in Chicago, Joseph Pulitzer in New York (who left $500,000 to the Philharmonic in 1911), were all inspired by the Major's example. The history of orchestral financing was a movement in which pioneering musicians might found an orchestra, but a few or one wealthy patron then subsidized it. It was later that the general public would be called on to support it.

But it was in the transition from subsidization to public support that the progression seemed to bog down. Even in the 1960s symphony orchestras were still considered preserves for aristocrats, not cultural necessities for the multitudes. During the growing years, no one—including Higginson—had thought through the question whether a symphony orchestra could ever have universal appeal. And as of this writing a workable solution is still to be advanced.

And yet, having said this and remarked on the prosaic qualities of the Major's thinking, it is clear that he did as much for American musicians as a host of union organizers. Higginson's BSO set standards, created interest in the symphonic literature, provided the experience by which orchestras throughout the nation were formed. Its success wrought far-reaching changes in the professionalism musicians demanded of themselves and far-reaching changes in the attitude the public took toward orchestral musicians. It led directly to the symphony orchestra with a fifty-two-week season, a phenomenon of the 1960s in America. Higginson's subsidized orchestra was one of Boston's greatest achievements.

# VI. *A Luxury for the Wealthy*

*"Music is a luxury for the wealthy. . . ."*
—Boston Gazette, *February 25, 1888*

## 1. *People with only money*

EARLY IN THE 1890s Mrs. William Astor and Mr. Ward
McAllister deemed it fashionable for elite New Yorkers to
be seen at the Metropolitan Opera House on Monday nights,
and socialites fought each other for boxes priced as high
as $30,000 each. Mrs. Astor, the frustrated wife of a millionaire
with penchants for horses, cruises and other women, aspired
to be the undisputed queen of New York society. McAllister,
the husband of a millionairess, aspired to limit the number
of local aristocrats to a group manageable by Mrs. Astor and
himself.

"There are only 400 people in fashionable New York
Society . . . ," McAllister confided to a *Tribune* reporter in
1888. "If you go outside that number, you strike people who
are either not at ease in a ballroom or else make other people
not at ease." McAllister was not quite sure himself who rated
inclusion in the "400" but was furious when Joseph Pulitzer's
*World* published its version of the upper crust, listing only
150 names. He subsequently published his own list in the
*Times* in February 1892. It included only 265 people. Later

he expanded it to 313, the closest it ever got to 400. In both his versions the base was Protestant Anglo-Saxon bankers, brokers, businessmen and members of families of inherited wealth.

McAllister considered it his sacred duty to guard Society and the Metropolitan against "profiteers, boorish people, people with only money," implying that he meant Jews, whom he excluded from his list, despite the fact that there were wealthy Sephardic Jewish families in New York that dated back to Dutch rule. Some Sephardim noted that their names were missing and expressed relief. Others were deeply perturbed. Rejection was blamed not on McAllister but on the actions of "loud, aggressive, new-rich" German-Jewish immigrants such as the Seligmans, the Lehmans, the Kuhns and the Loebs, many of whom had been peddlers and cloak-and-suiters before they became bankers on Wall Street. Thought to lack finesse and elegance, the newcomers were avoided by the Sephardim as well as by McAllister and the "400."

Kuhn, Loeb and Company, established in 1867 by two brothers-in-law, Abraham Kuhn and Solomon Loeb (previously cloak-and-suiters in Cincinnati), was typical of the new Jewish firms on Wall Street. Its five hard-working partners—all relatives—financed manufacturers and merchants. In 1875 they acquired Jacob Schiff, an orthodox Jew from Germany with an incredible talent for buying into railroads. Under Schiff's stewardship Kuhn, Loeb achieved a preeminence among American investment houses surpassed only by J. P. Morgan and Company. Schiff's success in negotiating financing for the transportation industry put the firm in a predominant position that was not affected until 1944, when the Interstate Commerce Commission required public sealed bidding for railroad securities.

Excluded from the social establishment, the partners founded a tight community of their own; like other Jewish establishments Kuhn, Loeb was under the control of "family." Non-relatives were not given positions of authority. Schiff married

Loeb's eldest daughter, Therese, and in the following genera-
tion partners' children married each other. Unless a partner's
daughter was available, an ambitious young executive without
blood ties had no avenue to a lofty job in the firm. Outside
talent was sought only for secondary tasks.

In 1896 a handsome twenty-nine-year-old banker named
Otto H. Kahn arrived at Kuhn, Loeb after previous banking
experience in London, where he frequented the best salons,
theaters and art galleries. Kahn, no cloak-and-suiter, was born
in Mannheim, Germany, and received an education in music,
art, poetry and theater as well as business. He favored the
artistic life and had little interest in religion, an attitude that
dismayed Schiff. Kahn was an erudite, charming, cosmopolitan,
suave financier who venerated singers, poets and artists, hob-
nobbed with the social elite whether Jewish or gentile, and
did not quite fit with devout types. He was to see himself as
"the flyleaf between the Old and New Testaments."

Kahn's swift rise to eminence on Wall Street is legendary.
He was soon one of Kuhn, Loeb's foremost experts on railroad financing and on January 1, 1897, a partner in the firm.
The success has been attributed to his energy, intelligence,
erudition, intuition, talent for detail work, aggressiveness and
buoyant self-confidence—that and his marriage in 1896 to
Adelaide Wolff, daughter of Abraham Wolff, one of the
original Kuhn, Loeb partners. At once Kahn was made a
prince of the realm, an intimate of the inner circle.

The Kahns dutifully took residence with the elder Wolff
in his Morristown, New Jersey, mansion, and Kahn busied
himself with Kuhn, Loeb and with one of its major clients,
Edward Harriman, the railroad tycoon. Kahn's great fortune
is said to have been made during the years when he, Harriman
and Schiff gained control of the Northern Pacific, the Great
Northern and other railroad lines. Though radically different
in personalities and interests, Kahn, Schiff and Harriman
formed one of the great teams in American finance, equal in
every way to such titans as James J. Hill and J. P. Morgan.

Mrs. Astor's society did not permit such as the Kahns to own boxes at the opera, but Jews were permitted to buy stock in the Metropolitan Opera and Real Estate Company, the shareholding company that owned the opera house, and to sit on its board. In 1903 Schiff was invited to join the august body. Schiff's interests ran strictly to business, his co-religionists and his philanthropies. He declined the invitation and recommended Kahn. Kahn, who often disconcerted Schiff by singing at the office, worried that identification with art might affect his reputation as a businessman. He took the problem to Edward Harriman, who, like Schiff, had no interest in opera but offered sage counsel: "You just go ahead and do your art job, but don't *dabble* at it. Make it one of your serious occupations. As long as you do not let it interfere with your other work, with your business duties and ambitions and thoughts, it will do you no harm. On the contrary, it will exercise your imagination and diversify your activities. It ought to make a better businessman out of you."

Thus encouraged, Otto Kahn bought two hundred shares of stock in the Metropolitan Opera and Real Estate Company. A Kuhn, Loeb client, James Hazen Hyde, sold him another three hundred shares. Henry Morgenthau, retiring from the board, provided an additional three hundred. Kahn took Harriman's advice seriously and bought all the stock he could obtain, eventually holding 2,750 shares. This made him the company's leading stockholder and a great favorite of the "400," but it was not enough to allow him to buy a box at the Metropolitan Opera House for Monday nights.

## 2. *The so-called opera house*

Kahn joined the Metropolitan board just as Maurice Grau announced his resignation. To replace Grau, directors chose a manager who knew little about opera, a custom of the house. Heinrich Conried had been an actor in his native Vienna and was the manager of a German theater on Irving Place in New York. He also sold steamer chairs to the Hamburg-America Line. Conried was a neophyte in crucial matters of repertory, casting and opera-house management. He was a plump impresario who hailed himself as "Rejuvenator of the Opera" and boasted that he could get along without stars, the day of his appointment. "I warrant I can put a star on one night and an ensemble opera the next and draw as great a crowd . . . ," he said.

Standing foursquare for opera without financial loss, Conried earned profits of $297,344 during his first three seasons at the Metropolitan. During his fourth, 1906–07, he lost $84,039. This was in large measure because of the San Francisco earthquake in which the Conried Metropolitan Opera Company troupe, then on tour, lost instruments, parts and costumes. In the 1907–08 season, his fifth at the house, Conried suffered a more grievous loss—$95,806. This was not because of a natural disaster but because of competition with a short, stout, industrialist-turned-impresario named Oscar Hammerstein, whose outstanding achievement to date was the invention of a mold for the manufacture of cigars.

Oscar Hammerstein was an opera fan so obsessed with the French and the Italian repertory that he was willing to sacrifice family, friends and fortune to manage an opera troupe. He loathed Conried because he believed that Conried catered to "official wealth" (*i.e.*, McAllister's "400"). He also loathed Conried because he thought Conried mismanaged the production of spectacles, an even deadlier sin in the eyes of so devoted a music lover.

For several years Hammerstein had nurtured plans to present opera to the multitudes, a concept in keeping with his desire to avoid contact with the "400." He entertained the sanguinary beliefs that the sale of tickets could alone support a modern house and that additional help from the rich in the form of gifts and high-priced subscriptions was unnecessary. This attitude stemmed largely from his inexperience. Hammerstein had never mounted a full season of opera with international stars. He had noted, however, the tremendous growth in New York's population (from 2,507,414 in 1890 to 4,766,883 in 1910) and the fact that the city's theaters seemed to be jammed no matter how good or bad a show was.

At the Metropolitan Opera House, Conried was shocked partly by Hammerstein's thinking but mostly by his announcement in February 1906 that the construction of a new house, the Manhattan Opera House, would shortly begin on a site between Eighth and Ninth avenues on Thirty-Fourth Street, five blocks away from the Metropolitan. Conried scoffed at Hammerstein's house as "the so-called opera house" on Thirty-Fourth Street. "I have not been urged to greater endeavor by the fact that there will be a rival in the field," the Rejuvenator told the press in advance of the 1906–07 season. "I have gone ahead with only one idea, and that was to get the best. New York isn't satisfied with anything but the best. . . ."

The Manhattan opened on December 3, 1906, and there was immediate doubt where the best was, at least musically. "While the world of fashion went to the Metropolitan . . . the musical people found their way to the Manhattan Opera House . . . ," said the *Times*. "The auditorium is designed for seeing and hearing, but not for the display of jewels and gowns." Like the other papers the *Times* lauded Hammerstein's principals, chorus and orchestra for their performances in Bellini's *I Puritani*. Conductor Cleofonte Campanini was said to have made "the most of the climaxes and [accompanied] the singers with the deepest sympathetic feeling," a sharp contrast with performances at the Metropolitan.

At the end of the second act, Hammerstein came on stage to make a speech. "I can only say that this is an effort toward furtherance of industry and music," he said. Still, he felt "compelled to add" that he was "the only one who has created this institution. I have had no assistance, financially or morally. The burden has all been on me and the responsibility is all mine. I have no board of directors, nobody to tell me what I should and should not do."

The barbs were obviously aimed at Conried and the Metropolitan and everyone in the large audience laughed. Everyone, that is, with the probable exception of the party in Box 13, which included Mr. and Mrs. Otto H. Kahn and Eliot Gregory, another Metropolitan director.

### 3. *The usual questions*

Oscar Hammerstein, who had no formal musical training, ran the Manhattan Opera House in ways no financier, impresario or musician had yet dreamed possible. In his haste to present opera to the masses, he disdained budgets, advance planning and dress rehearsals. His contempt for the rich was implacable. "Tell Clarence Mackay to go to hell," he told his son after learning that Mackay, the Atlantic cable and telegraph tycoon, was willing to help him financially. In advance of a season, a reporter inquired, "What do you intend to open the house with?" "With debts, I always open a house with debts," answered the impresario.

Despite such jollities Hammerstein mounted the grandest works of the repertory and presented the American premieres of Charpentier's *Louise*, Debussy's *Pelléas et Mélisande* and Strauss' *Elektra*. Nellie Melba, Luisa Tetrazzini and Mary Garden were among his prima donnas, all brilliant and none enjoying the security of dress rehearsals. Nor, according to Miss Garden, did the impresario trouble her with the "usual questions about what operas you've sung and how much money you want, and with whom you studied," when he engaged her. Instead he asked to see her figure.

Seated casually on a kitchen chair backstage at the Manhattan, Hammerstein deliberately scheduled performances the same nights as Metropolitan Opera performances, pitted his stars against Conried's stars, and worked prodigious hours in a crusade against the Metropolitan, "official wealth" and Conried. He insisted on realistic stage settings, intelligent stage direction and the closest possible cooperation between conductor and stars—features absent at the Metropolitan. He gave the best he had and he inspired others to give their best. This feature was likewise missing at the Metropolitan.

Hammerstein's immense daring won the admiration of press and public alike. Many marveled that he dared challenge the giants of New York society at all. Again and again Conried tried to lure Hammerstein's artists away with more lucrative contracts. Again and again, Conried succeeded. Hammerstein merely recruited others of the first rank to replace them.

So maddening was Hammerstein's success that Kahn took full charge at the Metropolitan Opera House on behalf of society, dispatching notes to the staff on matters large and small. Kahn had long since personally attended to casting and repertory problems. He suggested Enrico Caruso for Donizetti's *L'Elisir d'Amore* during Conried's first season (a brilliant success for the tenor), and he is said to have been involved in the decision to produce the American premiere of *Parsifal* in December 1904. He spared his fellow directors major responsibilities, made up deficits himself and was elected chairman of the board of directors of the Metropolitan in 1907.

Responsibility for failures was safely assigned to Conried. An example is the Metropolitan premiere of Richard Strauss' *Salome* during the 1907–08 season. A "strange horror or disgust" came over the opening-night audience after Salome's Dance of the Seven Veils. Metropolitan directors, likewise shaken, forbade additional representations. Kahn, a Strauss admirer, righteously advised the press that the house would "not be run again as it was this season." (Then he wrote Strauss and asked him not to assign the American rights for *Elektra* to Hammerstein.)

Kahn attempted to overwhelm Hammerstein with new stars, with new operas and, when all else failed, he fired Conried and hired a new manager, Guilio Gatti-Casazza. Six feet three of handsome, cultured Italian manhood, Gatti came to the Metropolitan Opera Company, a new corporate entity, from

La Scala, the mecca of opera devotees. He was the opposite of Hammerstein in all important respects except devotion to opera. Gatti was calm where Hammerstein was excitable, meticulous where Hammerstein was impulsive. He was the first manager at the Metropolitan to be employed on a completely salaried basis. It is said that Gatti and his wife would refuse to dine from a table that was not liberally sprinkled with rose petals.

Oscar Hammerstein, who ate on the run, treated Gatti with the same contempt as had warmed his relationship with Conried.

#### 4. *The only real impresario*

The observer seeking for clarity of thought in the Metropolitan-Manhattan confrontation, the worst operatic war in New York's history, is struck at once by its absence in either camp. Kahn, who would not be offered a box of his own at the Metropolitan Opera House until 1917, sat in Hammerstein's own box, as a guest, for the opening of the Manhattan Opera's third season. Kahn gave about $100,000 a year to the Met for the right of exclusion. Kahn, who was to call for culture for the masses, tried to forestall attempted Hammerstein operatic projects in Philadelphia, Baltimore and Chicago, cities that had no permanent opera troupes.

At the Manhattan, Hammerstein worked diligently to drive the rich shrieking in retreat from his house. In spite of his best efforts, younger members of New York society were attending regularly. Hammerstein finally succeeded in insulting Mrs. Clarence Mackay, early in January 1909. Mrs. Mackay helped sell 30 percent to 40 percent of all subscriptions for box and orchestra seats. She was told never again to set foot in the Manhattan after she neglected to send a note of gratitude to Hammerstein for use of the Manhattan Opera Orchestra at a private soirée. Society was shocked by the affront. Loyal to its own, it abandoned the impresario.

Hammerstein happily removed the Grand Tier boxes and added four rows of chairs for use by the general public. The season ended with his promise to operagoers of "forty grand operas and twenty-two grand opéra comiques in my repertory [the following season]. So New York may tremble. I thank you."

Midway in the following season—on January 1, 1910—a *Times* report possibly made Gatti tremble with news that Metropolitan Opera Company directors were considering Hammerstein, his archenemy, for the position of director of French opera at the Metropolitan. The newspaper's source was Hammerstein's son, Arthur. Next day a Metropolitan director privately denied that any such arrangement was being contemplated. On January 4, at 6 P.M., the entire board of directors issued a press statement categorically denying any negotiations between the rival houses.

At 8 P.M. the same evening, however, Arthur Hammerstein issued a statement at a press conference on his lengthy negotiations with chairman Otto H. Kahn concerning a possible merger of the Metropolitan and the Manhattan.

These negotiations, said Arthur, had begun early in December 1908 when he met with Kahn to discuss an understanding by which both houses could restrict the demands that singers were making for higher fees. Arthur found Kahn discouraged not only by greedy artists but by the situation at the Metropolitan. Gatti-Casazza was feuding with Andreas Dippel, a co-manager installed through the efforts of J. P. Morgan and other Metropolitan boxholders. Kahn called Oscar Hammerstein "the only real impresario in the field" and said that he would nominate him as general manager of the Metropolitan to the board of directors.

Hammerstein's name was duly submitted and, with the exception of William K. Vanderbilt, Sr., directors were in favor of the appointment. Kahn was to pursue the matter as late as November 1909, but no final decision was made, and he proceeded to offer an alternative, a merger of the two houses. There was more opposition to a merger than to Hammerstein alone, and in December Kahn told Arthur that all plans would have to be held in abeyance.

Meanwhile, without the support of the carriage trade, business had fallen off badly at the Manhattan Opera House. Hammerstein, who liked to take operagoers into his confidence, told audiences he might be forced to replace operatic productions with vaudeville acts. Yet he went on lavishing money on productions.

While Kahn was promoting Hammerstein at the Metropolitan, Lee Shubert, of the prominent family of theater owners, was promoting the Metropolitan at the Manhattan. In December Shubert told Arthur that directors at the Metropolitan had authorized him to negotiate for purchase of the Manhattan Opera House. In January 1910 Shubert suddenly modified his story; his purpose was not to buy out Hammerstein, only to buy an interest in the Manhattan.

Kahn's resolution of this situation, by December 1908 almost completely confused by claims, counterclaims and counter counterclaims, was one of his great achievements on behalf of the Metropolitan. Simply put, he bought off Hammerstein, with Arthur as the go-between. In mid-April 1910 Arthur convinced his father to sign a document giving him power of attorney. The day after, the elder Hammerstein quietly departed for Europe.

Ten days later, in Kahn's palatial residence on Fifth Avenue, Arthur used his power of attorney to sell his father's operatic interests to representatives of the Metropolitan. It was agreed that neither Oscar nor Arthur would present opera in the United States for a period of ten years. Further, that they would give over operatic properties and abandon projects in Chicago, Philadelphia and Boston, as well as in New York.

The Hammersteins received $1,200,000. Though the donor's name was a well-kept secret, it is generally thought today that the entire sum came from Kahn, who thus played St. George slaying the dragon for the Metropolitan. Not that the dragon was dead. Oscar Hammerstein eagerly looked forward to April 26, 1920, when he could again challenge the Metropolitan. But the chance never came. The impresario died in August 1919.

### 5. *A great cultural and artistic development*

Always racing the clock, Otto Kahn needed only four hours of each twenty-four for sleep. The remaining twenty were devoted to Kuhn, Loeb, and to theater, opera, ballet and art. Kahn kept to a split-second schedule as he dashed to the Metropolitan from his office, to the golf course, to parties, to his homes, always relying on his Cartier wristwatch for accuracy. Newspaper reporters got exactly five minutes for interviews; golf matches began precisely at 10:27 A.M. Caruso earned $10,000 to sing exactly two songs at his daughter Margaret's debut.

The diversity of Kahn's activities was such as to befuddle his contemporaries. Almost daily he established new records for largesse to the arts. His art collection included Corots, Rembrandts, Bouchers. His Long Island estate at Cold Spring Harbor resounded with the joyful shouts of subsidized actors, actresses, musicians, writers and painters. Occasionally he was himself befuddled. The financier invested $100,000 in a play; after it closed he realized that he had yet to learn its title.

Otto Kahn, a hero-worshiper and the object of worship by a coterie (or "zoo" according to Adelaide Kahn), scanned New York's newspapers and magazines daily for mention of his name. He hired a public relations firm, Ivy Lee, to keep the press properly informed of his gifts. No creative field was immune to his benefactions. New York was said, in one syndicated article, to be "a town frequently mentioned in connection with the name of Kahn."

"In this vast country there lies the raw material of a great cultural and artistic development," Kahn told admirers, and he saw it as his mission to bring art to the masses, a mission that had lately inspired Hammerstein. Kahn strove to become a one-man ministry of the arts, a financier encouraging everything worth encouraging. "I love anything that is beautiful," he said. "A beautiful building thrills me, a beautiful painting, a beautiful statue or a book, a beautiful meal, a beautiful woman."

To list Kahn's benefactions during the years between 1909 and 1929 is to note the period's cultural highpoints. Kahn subsidized the dance team of Anna Pavlova and Mikhail Mordkin and imported the Ballet Russe de Monte Carlo. To New York he brought France's Théâtre du Vieux Colombier and Théâtre de l'Odéon, Russia's Moscow Art Theatre and Germany's Max Reinhardt. He helped support the original Provincetown Players when they came to Greenwich Village and their most illustrious playwright, Eugene O'Neill. He contributed to the Habima Players and he presented the Abbey Players of Dublin. He was a friend and confidant of Theodore Dreiser and of Thomas Mann. He told George Gershwin he would have to "suffer" before he could produce a masterpiece.

Kahn was a modern Maecenas who wrote that it was a sin to keep money idle, but preached economy to his children and told his sister, whom he supported, to "adjust your way of living to match your income." He read everything from the classics to Ursula Parrot and took the subway so that he could enjoy the feeling of surging humanity. Despite his sophistication, he could seriously misjudge people. He backed Harding and supported Mussolini, though he later changed opinions about both men.

Kahn also thought about becoming a Catholic. In the 1920s a number of Seligmans had already taken the lead in becoming Methodists, Episcopalians and Roman Catholics, and mixed marriages were popular. When Jacob Schiff, the grand patriarch, died in September 1920, "Our Crowd" unbent. Without Schiff's forbidding mien to frighten lesser spirits, thoughts about conversion became more common.

Kahn saw St. Paul, St. Francis and Jesus as the "three

greatest figures of history" and regularly attended Holy Week services. He began to "play down" his Jewish background. In this he was not alone. Will Guggenheim, Adolph Lewisohn's son, Julius, and Joseph Seligman's grandson, Joseph II, had doubts that they were Jewish to begin with.

## 6. *We could astonish the world*

The day after Guilio Gatti-Casazza arrived in New York in 1908, Kahn asked him what he thought of the Metropolitan Opera House. "The auditorium pleased me a great deal," responded Gatti. "I find that it represents a rather happy compromise between the old opera house and the new. I don't think anything better could be imagined."

But, warming to the opportunity, Gatti began to enumerate defects noted during a brief visit to the Metropolitan the previous afternoon. Seats in the orchestra, the boxes, the dress circle and the two balconies were too near the stage on the sides, and the stage was too short and too narrow. There was a shortage of modern equipment, rehearsal rooms and storage facilities. "If one takes into consideration the length of the season and the riches of the repertoire, certainly the Metropolitan is an opera house that leaves much to be desired," Gatti concluded.

"Well, dear Mr. Gatti," Kahn answered, "what you say is perfectly true, and we have noticed these things before you. But don't worry about it and have patience. In two or three years a new Metropolitan Opera House will be built, answering all needs." Kahn instructed Gatti to make only those changes that would be "most useful."

This was patently impossible, since any useful change meant rebuilding at least part of the house. The inadequacies cited by Gatti were not the only ones that could be listed. Indeed, the most glaring inadequacy was the lack of low-priced seats. Moreover, because of poor design, those who sat in the balconies often faced a pillar or each other and could not see the stage. Operagoers of modest income were handicapped. Opera in New York continued to be more a private sport for the rich than a public art.

Conried, a staunch believer in the merits of the rich, had already convinced Metropolitan patrons to spend an estimated $3,000,000 to build the New Theatre, a structure on Central Park West and Sixty-First Street. Begun in 1907 and completed in time for the 1909–10 season, the New Theatre was intended primarily for intimate works such as plays and opéras comique. Its presentations attracted neither the rich nor the poor. Located in a neighborhood considered socially inferior, it had a preponderance of boxes that mediated against the very intimacy it was supposed to encourage. In 1911 it was leased to a theatrical producer, and the Metropolitan abandoned the New Theatre for a second opéra-comique company.

Kahn served on the New Theatre building committee and helped choose the architects who designed it. He also provided $50,000 of its capitalization. Despite his close connection, he admitted that the house was stifled in "heavy, golden raiment" and served up a "diet seasoned with 'society' ingredients."

How to open the Metropolitan Opera House to all New Yorkers concerned Kahn, especially after the demise of the New Theatre and the departure of Hammerstein. America was not the land of the "almighty dollar" but a country rich in artistic talent, thought Kahn. In a monograph, *Some Observations on Art in America,* he called on "we" to "give to art that full scope and place and honor to which it is entitled." Kahn also wrote that "we shall, I am convinced, astonish the world and ourselves by the greatness and intensity of the manifestation of the American spirit in art."

In August 1924 "we" got a specific assignment. Kahn returned to New York from an eight-week European trip and publicly called for the construction of a new Metropolitan Opera House. The limited accommodations of the old one, he said, denied the pleasures of opera to the many music lovers who could not afford to pay high prices for seats.

The Metropolitan Opera was duty-bound to provide "amply and generously for music lovers of small or modest means." It was a "semi-public institution."

Kahn's campaign for a new house began typically Kahn style with a substantial gift, a plot between Fifty-Sixth and Fifty-Seventh streets on Ninth Avenue, two blocks west of Carnegie Hall. Doubting any opposition from fellow directors, the financier further proceeded to negotiate a $1.7 million loan for construction from the Metropolitan Life Insurance Company. Kahn told reporters that clearance of the site would begin in January 1927.

The philanthropist was the hero of music critics, who found his site perfect, easily accessible by all forms of public transportation including elevated lines and subways. *Time* magazine delivered the ultimate accolade: a portrait of Kahn on the November 2, 1925, cover and profiles of him and Gatti inside the magazine.

Less enthusiastic was R. Fulton Cutting, chairman of the board of directors of the Metropolitan Opera and Real Estate Company, which actually owned the Thirty-Ninth Street house. "If the music lovers of New York wish a new home for opera, they are entitled to have one," he said generously in a public letter to Kahn. "The trustees of the present property . . . are not, however, of the opinion that the present building is antiquated or that its site is undesirable." Cutting added that if a new building was needed "the company of which Mr. Kahn is Chairman" could pay for it.

Cheered on by *Time*, *The New Yorker*, *Musical America* and the newspapers, Kahn named Benjamin Wistar Morris and Joseph Urban architects for a new opera house. Morris had designed the Morgan Annex for the main division of the New York Public Library; Urban was designer of the Ziegfeld Theatre. It was undoubtedly thought that their combined talents would produce the finest house possible. And one of its features, according to Kahn, was to be an absence of owned boxes.

Kahn left for a European trip in February 1927 brimming

over with confidence, mainly because he had obtained the boxholders' approval for the 5,000-seat project. True, the boxholders were to form an ownership group in the new house after all, but in April it was announced that they were turning in their stock to provide funds for the construction of the new house.

Within six months, Kahn's plans were in disarray, his dream shattered, the project rent by two mighty arguments. First, Urban and Morris had quarreled over the design of the auditorium, Morris arguing for a traditional horseshoe of boxes, Urban arguing for a "democratic house" in which the ticket buyers would all face the stage instead of each other. The argument being unresolved, Kahn found two sets of plans awaiting him when he returned from his trip.

Worse was a resurgence of discontent among boxholders. There were mutterings that the Fifty-Seventh Street site was not so desirable after all, that more desirable sites existed at Fifth Avenue and 110th Street facing Central Park, at the old New Theatre site, or at several other locations. Reasons were trotted out to obfuscate the truth—Cutting and the boxholders saw no need to spend their money on opera for everyone.

In January 1928 Kahn reminded directors and boxholders that they had approved the opera house, its site and its financing "by the unanimous vote of the boards"—his own Metropolitan Opera Company and that of The Metropolitan Opera and Real Estate Company. He offered to hold the Fifty-Seventh Street plot for one or possibly two months longer. The gesture was gratuitous. A cabal led by Mrs. Cornelius Vanderbilt III, determined to force the issue, overthrew the vote with objections to "the commercial features of Mr. Kahn's scheme," probably meaning a tower that would have included premises that would be rented, thus giving the Metropolitan added income.

At the end of January, Kahn announced that his brokers had put the property on the market. The site was eventually

utilized for an apartment house, the Parc Vendome. In a
reorganization in the 1930s, a second mortgage Kahn held
was totally lost, however. At $1.6 million, it represented the
financier's largest single gift to the arts.

### 7. *A real treat*

As Irving Kolodin points out in *The Story of the Metropolitan Opera*, the failure to build a new opera house in
1927 was to cost New York dearly. Even Cutting found the
subject hard to drop. Kahn was to say he knew nothing about
plans, but attempts were made to include a Metropolitan
Opera House in the Rockefeller Center complex in 1928.
Again unwelcome realities intruded. The Metropolitan Opera
and Real Estate Company offered the Thirty-Ninth Street
property for sale at $13 million. Informed opinion said $8
million was too high an asking price. John D. Rockefeller,
Jr., was also unwilling to give stockholders their boxes rent-
free. He would have required them to build the theater and
then to pay him rent, both unwelcome commitments.

Discussions about the Rockefeller Center site continued into
1932. They were rendered academic as early as 1929, however,
with the onset of depression days. The Thirty-Ninth Street
building remained a home for opera in New York for the
following thirty-odd years. When a new house was finally
opened in 1967 it cost $47 million or more than ten times
as much as the $4.6 million Kahn had budgeted in 1927. By
that time many a prospective operagoer had despaired of ever
getting into the house, let alone sitting behind a pillar.

The Metropolitan was hard hit by economic conditions.
Under Kahn's guidance its income reached an all-time high
in the years between 1926 and 1929. By the beginning of the
1931–32 season retrenchment was necessary, and Gatti proposed that everyone in the company "voluntarily" reduce his
salary by 10 percent. Opposition to this request came from

the company's leading tenor and highest earner, Beniamino Gigli, and its unionized employees. Gatti said it was petty to raise questions of contracts and rights "at such a critical time," but his own salary had been doubled to $60,000 in 1928 and was further increased to $67,057 for the 1930–31 season, when the company itself took a loss of $322,231.

Kahn said "it is hell to be considered rich," at the peak of the depression, and blamed Republican "boosters" for the "appalling mess." In June 1933 he went to Washington and testified before a subcommittee of the Senate Committee on Banking and Currency. The subcommittee chairman, Senator Duncan Fletcher of Florida, said that "it was a real treat to get his philosophy on banking . . . [and to hear his] many new thoughts and splendid ideas." Thomas S. Lamont of J. P. Morgan and Company and Winthrop Aldrich of the Chase National Bank also praised the way Kahn portrayed bankers in a favorable light, and put the blame for economic disaster on the "buyer's tide." Meanwhile, the depression got worse.

Kahn, a veteran first-nighter, missed his first opening night at the Metropolitan on November 21, 1932, when the company began its shortest season—16 weeks—since 1903. A month before, he had retired as chairman of the board of the Metropolitan Opera Company, pleading business responsibilities as his reason. Gatti thought the move presaged loss of support from Society and was later proved correct; most subscription cancellations were in the higher-priced seats. During the same season, the masses were asked to send donations for continued operation of the new Metropolitan Opera Association on a nationwide Metropolitan Opera broadcast. Society was also asked to help, but the solicitation took a different form. A glamorous pageant was held, at which New York's couturiers outdid each other in designing and making costumes. What remained of the old "400" served as patrons and patronesses of the affair.

At this juncture some of the many lives of Otto Kahn seemed to abruptly change direction. He had been the most generous supporter of the Metropolitan Opera in its history; now he took less interest in its situation. His name did not even appear on the executive committee of the "Campaign to Save the Metropolitan Opera."

Kahn suddenly developed an interest in Jews and Judaism. He served as chairman of a campaign dinner for the Federation for the Support of Jewish Philanthropic Societies and told a dinner group that "This is the time for every one of us to heed the call of the blood which courses in his veins and loyally and proudly stand up and be counted with his fellow Jews." Jewish friends called it "Kahn's conversion."

Kahn was undoubtedly shocked by events in Hitler's Germany, but did not throw himself into major anti-Nazi efforts. He resigned from German-American organizations and forbade Moselle and Rhine wines at his dinner table. He also helped refugees. For someone as self-centered as Kahn, there were probably other reasons for the change in outlook on Judaism. At least one has been provided by Irving Kolodin in *The Story of the Metropolitan Opera*.

According to Kolodin, shortly after he resigned from the Metropolitan, Kahn spoke with Olin Downes, music critic of *The New York Times*. Kahn told Downes that it was a good thing for him and for the Metropolitan Opera Company that he was leaving his post. His fellow directors had been content to let him take responsibility as long as he did all the work. Only one or two had cooperated with him. If he had had more cooperation and greater support, he would have experimented more boldly with repertory and staging. Under the circumstances, he had pursued a conservative course designed to *"assure popular support of the Metropolitan performances"* (italics added).

Kahn added that the primary cause of this coolness to him was that he was Jewish, and directors "were not wholly favorable to having a Jew as the chairman of their Board of Directors."

Kahn, prototype of the assimilated Jew, prospective convert

to Christianity, thus came full circle at the Met. After twenty-nine years and unquestioned devotion he was still *persona non grata*. In the face of persistent discrimination—the denial of a box—he was silent. When finally given a box he made only a feeble gesture of defiance. Kahn said he would not occupy the box but would allow it to be used by foreign dignitaries visiting the city.

According to the author of a recent book on Jewish-American aristocrats, this constitutes a "grand gesture" containing "tolerance, wit and just the right touch of derision." To less philosophical temperaments it indicates a man anxious to remain in good standing with peers who can, with impunity, treat him with contempt. For all his gifts and press releases, Kahn was outside the inner circle. He could neither persuade nor impress his associates. Thus, whenever a decision was imminent that would cost his fellow board members time and money, it was almost inevitable that they would refuse to help him.

To the very end of his life in 1934, Kahn went on bestowing largesse on poet and proletariat alike, seeking popularity everywhere. His financial losses were estimated to have reached $50 million; he pushed himself mercilessly in pursuit of business and pleasure. Kahn continued to make the rounds in Europe and America, a somewhat anachronistic figure at a time when Jews were already running for their lives.

When Kahn died, condolences came from all over the world. One admirer wrote his widow that "he burned out his life in an eager effort to make his visions of a brighter life more real in service to the many." At the Metropolitan Opera House, *Parsifal*, an opera about a simpleminded knight, was given in his memory.

# PART THREE
## *Organizers*

# VII. *Wholesalers and Retailers*

*"The manager's function is changing. He no longer is merely a sales-man. He must be an advisor to the local manager, and the relationship between the wholesaler and retailer, as it were, must be cooperative."*

—ARTHUR JUDSON

*"An artist's greatness depends not only upon his possession of superior talent and ability but, perhaps, most important, upon his objective understanding of the audience on hand. . . . He must be able to over-come individual points of resistance, which some artists tell me they can spot instinctively."*

—O. O. BOTTORFF

## 1. *The musical stock market*

WHEN CONSIDERING the foibles of artists, audiences and man-agers in the period between the Civil War and World War I, the student of American musical life is apt to throw up his hands and remark that music making could never become a stable profession. To most Americans the word "musician" still connoted a "longhaired foreigner of doubtful morals." Even in the larger cities concertgoers were restive; during the 1880s and 1890s patrons frequently found notes in their programs beseeching "any one desirous of entering or leaving [this] concert [to] kindly do so between the pieces."

Artists of European celebrity found that previous experience did not necessarily fit them for American tours. "The moment I set foot on American soil I became a *hustler*," admitted Jean Gérardy, a Belgian cellist. The German violinist Carl Flesch, like many others, "stayed no longer than necessary" and booked a return passage on arrival. Joseph Joachim, one of the great violinists of all time, adamantly refused to tour the United States in the belief that his emphasis on musicianship rather than technical dexterity would be misunderstood.

But some virtuosi, notably pianist Moriz Rosenthal, gave as many as one hundred concerts a season and earned fortunes. "Don't you ever get sick of your technic?" an editor asked Rosenthal. "Does Vanderbilt get sick of his money?" retorted the performer.

It was found that a Slavic or Germanic name could be of crucial importance to an artistic career, and thus a pianist from Texas named Hickenlooper returned to the United States from a European trip renamed Olga Samaroff. Female artists were at a further disadvantage because it was commonly held that sin and the stage had a reciprocal causal relationship. The major exception to this prejudice was Adelina Patti. Though twice divorced, Patti earned fame, fortune and a castle in Wales, thanks to her clamorous fans and to her stubborn refusal to appear unless she was paid in advance of her performances.

Despite this muddle, increasing numbers of performers toured the United States. In answer to a need for specialization of duties, a new marketing system for artists also became prevalent during the late 1880s. Instead of a manager's assembling troupes and going along on a tour to produce performances—as had been done since the early days of the Republic—local sponsors (assisted by "artists' " managers in New York) rose to present musical attractions.

A leading example of the new breed of local promoter was L. E. Behymer, a Los Angeles resident who had arrived from Illinois in 1886 and was a merchant, laborer, usher, book reviewer and ticket scalper before embarking on a career as a musical retailer.

Behymer was determined to bring great music to Southern California. He was further determined to receive adequate financial remuneration for his many and good efforts. A "grasping mercenary," his enemies called him, but then Len Behymer never could resist tough campaigning when new territories beckoned or old ones were invaded by competitors. His first venture of consequence was the presentation of the

Maurice Grau Grand Opera Company in the fall of 1900. An indication of the respect in which his early promotions were held is an editorial in the *Los Angeles Graphic* in 1905 advising that "a dozen times he has been knocked out by the refusal of Angelenos to recognize the worth of the musical attractions he has brought here, but every time 'Bee' [Behymer] has come up smiling, to try once more."

Emboldened by editorial praise and blessed with an indomitable ego, Behymer told Angelenos the following year that the city stood in danger of "musical collapse" unless it rallied to the support of his presentations. While the citizenry contemplated imminent cultural decline, he organized the Great Western Lyceum and Concert Bureau, which supplied musical and lecture talent to cities and towns in twelve Western states. The impresario sent publicity as far as Fresno and Phoenix for a performance of *Parsifal*, which was given for the first time in Los Angeles by the Conried Metropolitan Opera Company in 1905. "It makes no difference whether one is fashionable or unfashionable at so solemn and exceptional a function as a 'Parsifal' performance," he told customers who wondered whether the same dress could properly be worn for an opera divided into an afternoon and evening presentation. "What does it matter so you see 'Parsifal'—probably your only chance in a lifetime."

Nearly half a century later, Behymer was supplying artists to audiences in the entire Southwest as well as to California and other West Coast states; before he died in 1947, he would also manage the Los Angeles Philharmonic Orchestra and the Hollywood Bowl. The "Busy Bee," a one-man agency, was hailed as the "daddy" of all local managers by no less than Sol Hurok.

While Behymer and other local managers nurtured audiences in the hinterlands, artists' managers in the East fostered the careers of budding and established performers. Perhaps the most distinguished member of this fraternity was Charles A. Ellis, whose agency flourished in the 1890s and early 1900s and whose clients included Melba, Paderewski, Kreisler, Farrar and Samaroff. Ellis, who was also manager of the Boston Symphony Orchestra, handled his affairs without benefit of a large office or staff, preferring to keep things moving while on the fly. "The Lord helps those that help themselves," he claimed. Ellis cajoled local managers into giving him the highest fees possible for musicians on his roster.

Because he accepted relatively few artists as clients, and most of those already famous, Ellis was able to devote much thought to the problems of each. He established a reputation for equable temperament, integrity and keen artistic judgment that has since been matched by few other managers. "A contract with Ellis was . . . an open sesame in the American concert world . . . ," said Olga Samaroff, who was happy to find that he demanded no money in advance for promotion when he offered her a contract.

Unlike other managers, Ellis did not overload his roster with child prodigies, coloratura sopranos and instrumentalists with flashy techniques. Still he demanded of each performer some quirk of personality or career that would pique the curiosity of a nonmusical public. He could not be induced to manage an artist if he did not have faith in the performer's ability. "Some local managers have told me that 'Ellis artists' are considered to be 'gilt-edged' securities in the musical stock market," Olga Samaroff wrote her father, a businessman who could not quite get the hang of the concert business. "In spite of all the overhead expenses . . . my contract with Ellis is the best any artist could have. . . . A letter from him can procure an engagement without the persuasive activities of a road agent."

New York remained the nation's musical headquarters, and its leading artists' manager was Henry Wolfsohn, head of the Wolfsohn Musical Bureau. Wolfsohn advised Mme. Samaroff that "if you played like Liszt and Rubinstein rolled into one, I could do nothing for you in this country without European prestige [*i.e.*, press notices]." Wolfsohn managed her debut, which cost her a four-figure sum, and then asked for $5,000 in promotion money to advance her career.

Unlike Ellis, Wolfsohn employed a large staff of road agents who traveled the country ceaselessly selling artists to local sponsors and to music clubs. He welcomed both famous and unknown artists to his list, since any and all commissions helped pay for the office overhead. Wolfsohn's clients included such notables as Ernö von Dohnányi and Maud Powell. He displayed no great personal interest in the musical virtues of any of his artists, but when he died in 1909 he was, ironically, in the midst of negotiations to bring one of the greatest musicians of the time, Sergei Rachmaninoff, to the United States for a fee of $250 per concert.

The 1890s and early 1900s saw the emergence of trusts in almost every business field, and managers in New York felt keenly the lack of organization in their own field. Lyceum bureaus, usually concerned with less esoteric talents, had begun cutting into their business. In 1907 an artists and concert managers trust was proposed, and it was rumored that a circuit of concert halls would be among the first projects of the chartered corporation. The plans collapsed in the face of fears that governmental investigation—then underway in other business fields—would follow immediately on establishment of a circuit.

Fourteen years later, in December 1921, a convention of the National Association of Concert Managers heard "a scheme for dividing the entire country into thirteen districts with a member of the Concert Managers' Association at the head of each district. . . ." Musical performances would be scheduled in a more orderly fashion, and ticket prices could be lowered. "Five dollar opera," said President Walter Fritschy, "is absurd."

It probably was, but Fritschy's association was beginning to organize audiences a little too late.

## 2. *Just follow the plan*

In the fall of 1920, Harry P. Harrison, general manager of the Redpath-Chicago Lyceum Bureau, found that he could not book engagements he had promised Charles Marshall, a rising Chicago Civic Opera tenor. Harrison supplied lecturers and entertainers to the entire Midwest. In a final attempt to obtain sufficient bookings for Marshall he recruited several artists and offered them and the tenor up as an "All-Star Series."

It was exceedingly risky to personally guarantee the artists' fees, and Harrison had no idea how lyceum customers would react to the prospect of an all-musical series. To cover costs, he decided to charge each lyceum in advance for his artists. This bold innovation did not deter customers, and the requisite number of sales was made. Thus encouraged, the entrepreneur formed a new agency in early 1921 for the express purpose of selling "All-Star Series." Harrison also acquired a partner, Dema Harshbarger, head saleswoman of the rival Century Lyceum Bureau.

Miss Harshbarger, who had long labored in Midwest lyceum circuits despite polio and rheumatic fever in earlier years, took it as her task to organize some audiences. In March 1921 she went to Battle Creek, Michigan, where she organized a "Civic Music Committee" that promptly bought a Harrison and Harshbarger "All-Star Series." Thirteen similar committees were formed by her during the next year in the Greater Chicago area. By 1930 she was to organize 182 "Civic Music Committees" in thirty-two states, each of which presented an annual series purchased from Harrison and Harshbarger.

Organizational tactics were the same everywhere. Miss Harshbarger first ascertained the names of the foremost citizens in the community. After enlisting them on a committee for good music and her series, a campaign was launched to secure as many subscribers as there were seats in the local auditorium. Single concert tickets were not sold. Either a music lover bought a prepaid subscription or he bought nothing. The one departure from Harrison's original procedure was that neither the names of artists nor the programs they would perform were announced in advance of the sale of tickets. Not until Miss Harshbarger and the volunteers knew how much money was actually collected was the talent chosen and booked.

In practice, a series usually consisted of a recital by one well-known artist and appearances by two or three lesser-known musicians, all of whom programmed "standard" works and semipopular pieces. Their services were obtained via Harrison and Harshbarger from offices in New York, where artists' managers were happy to get solid blocks of bookings from sponsors who would definitely not go bankrupt.

Harrison and Harshbarger took its fees from the pre-series receipts, and the plan was hailed everywhere as both economically foolproof and nonprofit, as indeed it was for the volunteers. "Harrison and Harshbarger have worked out a plan which is obviously sound and fair, and which obviates any possibility of financial loss," reads a Harrison and Harshbarger advertisement aimed at unorganized sponsors in 1922. "This has proved in practice to be one of the greatest ideas ever formulated in connection with the presentation of an artist series."

Besides Harrison and Harshbarger, those who thought well of the plan included Samuel Insull, a high-powered Chicagoan who headed a utilities empire and was a guarantor of the Chicago Civic Opera. Insull was worried that his artists might be lured away by the Metropolitan Opera in New York, and he wanted to offer them recital dates in addition to their operatic engagements. In 1925 he purchased a controlling interest in Harrison and Harshbarger to obtain a recital outlet, and he incorporated the firm under a new name, Civic Concert Service. This gave the agency more working capital and a change in policy—Chicago Civic Opera artists were favored—and Harrison took the opportunity to retire from active management. Miss Harshbarger remained and continued to pepper the Midwest with Civic Music Associations.

Meanwhile, in New York, Arthur Judson, an enterprising, handsome ex-*Musical America* reporter who took over the Wolfsohn concert management in 1928 and was manager of the Philadelphia Orchestra in 1922, proposed to six other New York artists' managers that they join him in organizing some audiences of their own. One reason was to solve the problem of tours on which there were layovers between dates in large cities, and, consequently, idle artists. Organized audiences could act as stepping-stones to these major engagements. Another reason, equally compelling, was to beat Miss Harshbarger and her zealous sales staff to Eastern markets.

Community Concerts Corporation, the new circuit, was headed by Sigmund Spaeth, a music critic and former sportswriter later to become famous as the "tune detective." Fifteen Northeastern cities were organized during its first year; within three years, forty-two cities and towns were in the fold. Unlike Civic, however, Community restricted the sources from which artists could be engaged. Every performer presented was on the roster of one of the seven founding managements.

This tight, profitable, cooperative effort continued even when Daniel Mayer, one of the Community founders, withdrew with his assistant, Marks Levine, to set up the National Broadcasting and Concert Bureau, an artists' management under the aegis of the National Broadcasting Company. The remaining Community founders organized a new cooperative artists' management, Columbia Concerts Corporation. It went along with the circuit, which was renamed Community Concert Service. In 1930 they joined the Columbia Broadcasting System. This was not an entirely fortuitous occurrence, since Judson was also a founder and stockholder in CBS.

Soon after its acquisition of artists' management and circuit,

CBS announced that it could not provide NBC with Community recital and concert outlets, and thus effectively removed its rival from competition in its territories. NBC then purchased an interest in Civic and, in 1935, bought the circuit outright, acquiring hundreds of organized audiences of its own. This last purchase marked the end of Dema Harshbarger's association with Civic. She quit Chicago for Hollywood, where her later accomplishments included teaming up Leopold Stokowski with Bing Crosby in movies and promoting Lum 'n Abner. Insull's connection had been severed three years earlier when he fled the country to Greece, one step ahead of Federal agents seeking to arrest him for allegedly using the mails to defraud.

The new alignments inspired a movement of experienced Civic salesmen to positions of power in the New York offices of both Civic and Community. Ward French, an ex-high school teacher, trumpet player and crack Harrison and Harshbarger salesman, became general manager of Community in 1930. O. O. Bottorff, a Chautauqua circuit salesman at sixteen and a Civic Concert Service salesman since 1928, joined NBC's agency in 1935. Seven years later, when NBC quit the concert field rather than face investigation by the Federal Trade Commission for monopolistic practices, Bottorff became co-owner of the agency (which was renamed National Concert and Artists Corporation) with Marks Levine. CBS divested itself of Columbia and Community for similar reasons in 1942, but both Judson and French remained at their posts, Judson as president of Columbia Artists Management, Inc., and French as president of Community Concert Service, Inc.

The Judson-French Columbia-Community combination and the Bottorff-Levine NCAC-Civic combinations were to endure for another thirteen years, a period in which 1,900 organized audiences came to rely on them, their representatives, and their organized audience plan, which continued to display the same characteristics as under Dema Harshbarger's direction. "Just follow the plan," a Community executive named Ben Lobdill told sponsors in a pamphlet issued during the early 1950s. "[It] is the infallible motto for difficult situations."

But some difficult situations began to arise for which neither the motto nor the plan seemed to offer much help. One such was artists' reactions to the fees received after they performed on the Community circuit. Kathleen Ferrier, the distinguished British soprano, wanted to know where, if the concerts were "non-profit making, the money went. I have an average of 3000 in the audience—which means at least 3000 dollars and they pay me 800, out of which I pay an accompanist 105—20 per cent manager's fees—rail travel for two (which is a colossal amount here) hotel, taxis, porters and tips—and income tax!"

This puzzler—just where *did* the money go—exercised the curiosity of organized audience association members, too, particularly after they heard about the "differential" which had to be paid by artists on all Community and Civic dates. The word "differential" was (and remains) a managerial colloquialism for the difference between the artist's fee and what he actually received from Community or Civic for his performance. If his fee was $400, for example, he might actually receive only $250, out of which he still had to pay his manager's commission, promotional costs, his accompanist's fee, both his transportation and his accompanist's transportation and his own accommodations. The other $150 went to Community or to Civic to pay for the operation of the circuits. Though the differential could go as high as 40 percent of an artist's gross fee, the American Guild of Musical Artists (which represents the artists) and artists' managements have agreed that it should never exceed 29 percent of the average fee of artists on their lists.

The differential was (and is) always an integral part of the organized audience plan—it supports both the representatives and the home offices—but news of it was not really bruited about until the 1940s when Miss Ferrier and other such artists themselves began to discuss it with increasing frequency. In 1945 Arthur Judson made one of the few oblique managerial references in print to commissions. A *Current Biography* article about him noted that "because the [organized audience] plan was instituted to benefit small-town music lovers," the money advanced by Columbia in 1930 to French for Community expansion was "a loan not to the communities but collectively to [Judson's] artist clients."

Judson's explanation for this collective repayment surprised those groaning under its weight. There was also collective surprise among some organized audience committees when they heard the size of the "loan"—$250,000. Cecil Smith, whose 1947 article in *The New Republic* did much to clarify the "differential" situation was in turn surprised when he "found that [Ward] French was perfectly willing not only to tell me all about the differential but to open all the corporation's books for my examination. . . ." An accountant was duly sent by Smith to French's office. Smith learned that "at that time all the artists understood about it before they signed their management contracts." To Smith, this somehow made it all right, and there were no further discussions with French about what would happen if an artist refused to pay a 29 percent differential. Indeed, the matter has hardly been discussed publicly since, and one can only surmise that artists, managers and organized audiences are satisfied with the arrangement.

But having faced up to both sponsors and artists, the circuits were soon to find themselves with a new batch of worries. During the late 1940s, the Department of Justice, which had previously shown little interest in music and musicians, was curious as to why 1,900 organized audiences throughout the country each seemed intent on engaging artists managed by the two parent organizations.

## 3. *Nolo contendere*

Until 1955, the exact number and location of organized audiences and the dates of annual sales campaigns were business secrets closely guarded by Civic and Community executives. There was little doubt that the vast majority of artists that appeared before organized audiences came from the rosters of Columbia and National Concert and Artists Corporation. It was estimated that the two firms booked performers for 85 to 90 percent of *all* concerts in the United States.

"Independent" artists' managers (*i.e.*, unaffiliated with Columbia or NCAC) were effectively blocked from the organized audience market by reason of the close relationship between Columbia and Community and NCAC and Civic. The independent manager could only hope to learn that a local committee had inquired about one of his artists, that a block of Community or Civic engagements was open because of an artist's cancellation or that Columbia or NCAC simply did not have the particular artist or type of group desired on their rosters, an unlikely possibility.

If a local association did want an artist managed by an independent, it faced objections from the circuit representatives who held forth for the engagement of artists from the parent offices. The result was that independent managements, many of them woefully undercapitalized, went out of business at an increasing rate during the 1950s. By the end of the decade, it seemed as if the field would soon shrink to the two giants, Columbia and NCAC.

The situation caused tensions within the giants as well as without. Thus Ward French rocked the organized audience world in 1954 with an announcement that he wanted local associations to have a "decent degree of independence" and "a free choice of artists." French went even further and called for the separation of Columbia and Community. He was immediately deposed as president of Community, but made plans to form a new circuit—plans that collapsed within a month. Instead of selling artists, French retired to the Virgin Islands to sell real estate. His successor, Frederick C. Schang, promptly addressed a letter to Community associations deploring the "French Revolution." French, said Schang, had been ousted from the board because "after twenty years' belief to the contrary, [he] urged the separation of Community Concerts, Inc., from the Columbia Artists Management," an incredible act of disloyalty.

Yet another ex-Community employee strongly in favor of the separation that Schang deplored was Kenneth Allen, a nephew of soprano Maggie Teyte, a World War II army captain and a Sherwin-Williams Paint Company heir. Allen represented Margaret Truman during her brief singing career in the late 1940s, when she was under the management of a firm owned jointly by himself and James A. Davidson. He and Davidson spoke with President Truman about conditions in the music world, and Truman called in the Federal Bureau of Investigation. When the FBI turned its findings over to the Department of Justice, a new administration had taken office and progress on the case began to lag. On October 20, 1955, however, a complaint was filed by the United States Government in the Southern District Court of New York against the circuits and their parent organizations.

"Beginning in or about 1933," the complaint charged, "and continuing thereafter to the date of the filing . . . the defendants [Civic, Columbia, Community and NCAC] have combined and conspired in unreasonable restraint of . . . interstate trade and commerce in the management and booking of artists and in the formation and maintenance of organized audience associations and have combined and conspired to monopolize, have attempted to monopolize, and have monopolized said trade and commerce in violation of Sections 1 and 2 of the Sherman Act. . . ."

It was alleged that Community and Civic had acted not only to exclude independent managers from contact with organized audience committees but had allocated "specified towns, cities and communities through the United States wherein each might set up and maintain organized audience associations without competition from the other." This was thought to account for a curious phenomenon that many had observed but few could explain—how it was that Community and Civic associations never seemed to operate side by side in the same towns and cities.

The four defendants pleaded *nolo contendere* (unwilling to contest the charges), paid fines totaling $26,000 and signed a "consent decree" under which Community and Civic promotional materials would henceforth include the artists rosters of independent managers in addition to the parent organizations' artists rosters.

For a year after the consent decree there was considerable promotional activity by the independents, and afterwards a fair number of bookings. Today, nearly a quarter of the recitals and a third of group performances on the Community circuit are given by artists from independent managements, a substantial improvement over the earlier situation.

Nonetheless the realities of the organized audience world remain harsh for independents. Without capital to hire a large sales force, the independent manager is at a disadvantage in competing with the efficient, far-flung empire that is Columbia Artists Management, now the largest agency in the nation. He cannot guarantee any but the most renowned artists the same volume of engagements year in and year out. Worse, he may develop an artist's career at considerable expense of time and effort only to lose the performer to Columbia when he has reached the higher levels of his profession.

One solution to these problems has been specialization, and thus some independents now devote themselves almost entirely to chamber music or to some other area of the field. The enormous rise in concerts in colleges and universities has encouraged this growth in specialized agencies, since the audiences are often more sophisticated than those along the regular concert trails. Though no one knows exactly how much colleges and universities spend for music, at least one independent management now acknowledges that 75 percent of its sales are made on campuses.

## 4. *S. Hurok presents*

One "independent" manager has regularly avoided almost every ill that besets fellow practitioners. While colleagues struggled vainly to obtain organized audience dates, he charged telephone and telegraph bills to NCAC, allowed it to pay his office rent and permitted it to do all his bookings. He spent his time searching for glamorous artists. Civic representatives had instructions to give them precedence. For these services he frequently paid Bottorff and Levine a commission on bookings as low as 7½ percent.

Sol Hurok did not think much of the "plan" itself. "The organized audience plan is destructive to music, not constructive," he said in 1957. "But you can't always blame the managers. They have built up . . . vast organizations . . . [and] they can't afford to lose that business."

Sol Hurok, the most famous impresario of modern times, sprang full-blown to international fame from the Brownsville section of Brooklyn, much as Athena is said to have sprung completely assembled from the head of Zeus.

Hurok arrived in the United States from Pogar, Russia, in May 1906 with three rubles and went to Philadelphia, where he bundled newspapers and served as a streetcar conductor. Later that year he moved to New York, where he sold hardware and peddled notions. About 1911, without special training in music or in management, he began supplying labor organizations and clubs in the Brownsville section of Brooklyn with musical talent. He ran through local celebrities quickly and then engaged Efrem Zimbalist, at that time a Big Name, for a concert. Zimbalist became the first artist of international reputation to appear under the Hurok aegis, albeit at a local house, Brownsville's New Palm Garden, and for the benefit of the Socialist Party.

By 1915, Hurok had managed a labor lyceum, presented concerts at the Brooklyn Academy of Music, organized the Van Hugo Musical Society and lost money on a series called "Music for the Masses" at the Fourteenth Regiment Armory in Brooklyn. He was soon to launch a successful series of Sunday-night concerts at "popular prices" (a $2 top) at the Hippodrome Theater in New York, to travel to Paris to engage Feodor Chaliapin for a tour (he would fail in this early attempt), and to manage an American tour by Anna Pavlova. Before reaching the age of thirty-two he was one of the foremost impresarios in New York, a masterful synthesis of talent, flamboyance and *chutzpah*.

This sudden leap from obscurity to eminence is explained not only by Hurok's capacity for hard work and his promotional talents (on a level with P. T. Barnum's), but by his need for recognition—a trait shared with other graduates of Brownsville, many of whom also occupy peaks in the business and entertainment worlds.

After half a century of praise and admiration, Hurok becomes unhappy if his name does not regularly appear in the newspapers and on the posters used to advertise concerts. By contractual agreement with local sponsors, the legend "S. Hurok Presents" must appear over artists' names on all promotional materials. The Hurok publicity office is attuned as much to the Chief as to the Product; although other impresarios have had articles written about them, Hurok is one of the few who rated a movie about his adventures. "When Hurok, enormous horn-rimmed glasses over his owl-like eyes, pushes his plump frontage into the Pavillon in New York . . . headwaiters and flunkies converge like a school of perch around a particularly succulent bait," writes critic Harold Schonberg of *The New York Times*. "Hurok gets what Ludwig Bemelmans calls the $10 headwaiter's bow (as against the $1 one), and this is the deepest one of all, reserved ordinarily for royalty and important Hollywood figures."

As befits a reigning monarch, Hurok has always stood

apart from other artists' managers, most of whom are in awe of his uncanny ability to invest exotic, glamorous and profitable attractions with yet more exoticism, glamor and profit.

During the early 1930s, when managers flocked to the radio networks, he remained an independent. At NCAC, Hurok supplied many of the greatest artists available; Levine supplied sales representatives and organized audiences. When NCAC and Civic were sold by Bottorff and Levine in 1955 to a baritone named Luben Vichey, Hurok went along with the new owner. But trouble loomed. Vichey resented his organization's having to do all the hard work of booking Hurok artists. "I do not know how it happened in the beginning years ago," Vichey said in *Variety*. "We collected perhaps $100,000 a year from Hurok, but in order to satisfy and serve him, all our regular field representatives had to give Hurok acts precedence. Nor could we compete with him for big units. Hurok was one part of a big organization. We have over 100 employees, over $750,000 in annual overhead, but Hurok was the tail that wagged the dog."

Having disgorged Hurok and his staff with considerable relief in 1957, NCAC and Civic promptly fell on evil days and began a downward plunge from which they have yet to recover in 1969. Hurok began a spectacular uphill climb, reaching new heights of success and adulation for his management of the Moiseyev Dancers, the Bolshoi Ballet, the Kirov Ballet and the Pipes and Drums, Regimental Band and Highland Dancers of the Black Watch.

Whether or not Hurok has accomplished these wonders of promotion with an eye to improving the musical commonweal is a point difficult to determine but easy to discuss at cocktail parties. *The New York Times* has said that he has accomplished "more for music in America than the invention of the phonograph." But Hurok has also been solidly in favor of the star system, which is probably detrimental in the long run to American musical life since it focuses public attention on the flashiest performers rather than on the music itself.

He gleefully admits to the charge. "Such is the present state of musical appreciation in this country that it is an open secret that in many cities the way to sell out, or nearly sell out, is to engage soloists with box-office appeal," he wrote in *Impresario*, an autobiography published in 1946. "It [is] my contention that the guest star principle [has] been responsible for American interest in ballet. I hope the reader will pardon me if I link that system, coupled with my own great enthusiasm, and faith in ballet, with the popularity that ballet has in this country today."

Doubtless, Hurok's "great enthusiasm," his great stars and his ability to do big things in a big way did bring on a major interest in ballet in America after World War II. ("Others have talents," Hurok has said. "Hurok has artists.") Equally important is his willingness to gamble and to take the consequences should the gamble go sour. A single season with Ballet Theatre cost him $85,000. In 1925, says Hurok, "I brought over the Russian Grand Opera and brought to it, Feodor Chaliapin himself. What a man! What a singer! It was a pleasure to present him with his opera company on a grand scale in Chicago. . . . Well, I lost maybe $150,000."

Back in New York after this last fiasco, the impresario retired to his hotel room and found that the key did not fit the lock, which was plugged. A brief discussion ensued with the clerk and manager about his unpaid hotel bill, and he was politely but firmly ejected from the premises. For several nights Hurok occupied Central Park benches, but "[I] kept my troubles to myself, kept my clothes in order as best I could, kept my office and my secretary at 55 West 42nd Street, and kept my ear to the ground for a chance to get started again."

The extent to which he succeeded in reestablishing his preeminence in a field uncharitable to fallen heroes is evident in the great artists he subsequently presented and in his lavish parties. (No frankfurter, herring and Scotch affairs these, but saturnalia that could, and do, cost up to $15,000.) Thanks to the Chaliapin fiasco, Hurok learned that he would have to curb his enthusiasm and "use other measuring rods for the public. In those days I wrote contracts the way a certain school of sentimental poets used to write verses: If the poet was melancholy rain was not rain, it was nature weeping. . . ."

The truest measure of his inventiveness, however, has not been what he could do for clients who were already established but what he could do for artists on the verge of stardom. Hurok's most famous triumph in this direction was the Marian Anderson concert at the Lincoln Memorial in Washington in 1939, an event that catapulted the Negro soprano to international fame, humbled the Daughters of the American Revolution and saw Hurok cast in the combined roles of impresario and social visionary. Without this dramatic performance, which he publicized after Anderson had been refused an appearance in the DAR's Constitution Hall, there is doubt that she would have attracted audiences so quickly. Similarly, Hurok's skill in bringing Victoria De Los Angeles to the fore after an unpromising debut, and in establishing an audience for Sadler's Wells Ballet in advance of its American debut (a triumph not unlike Barnum's for Jenny Lind) attests to his impressive professionalism. "An impresario," he says succinctly in *Impresario,* "does not make an artist. He makes an audience."

Hurok knows whom to promote, what to promote, when to promote, how to promote and where to promote. What he may not always know is when to stop promoting and start building permanent, solid organizations. Bursting with enterprise, he goes from group to group, some of which languish quickly after the first and lush periods of popularity are passed under his management.

He also admits that he is at least partly responsible for the decline in opportunities for solo performers. "There is the problem of the so-called 'group attractions' which have crowded so many solo performers out of the concert series," he said in *Musical America* in 1961. "I am not the least of-

fender in creating this market for numerous people instead
of one. . . ." The question, continued Hurok, "should always
be quality, not quantity. To believe that a crowd of inferior
performers is more interesting than one superb one, is a very
peculiar idea indeed." Yet by his hoopla and by the Holly-
wood-style promotions he gives his groups, Hurok has done
more than any other manager to inculcate this "peculiar idea"
in the minds of the American public.

## 5. *The music boom*

In 1963, more people attended concerts than attended base-
ball games, Community Concerts produced over 3,500 performances, the New York Philharmonic was about to become
the first American orchestra to offer its members a 52-week
season and the situation of the solo performer was so precarious that a conference of managers, artists and critics was
called by *Musical America* and AGMA, at the height of the
booking season, to decide what, if anything, could be done. In
the midst of the most highly publicized music boom in history
("a massive unstopping of the U. S. ear," *Time* called it),
hundreds of instrumentalists and singers, many with superior
abilities, found it impossible to secure enough engagements to
remain in the field.

That this simultaneous boom and bust occurred just as the
American musician was accepted as a useful member of
society and after forty years of organized audiences was not
the least ironic aspect of the situation. To cite two examples
of progress, in 1946 the Boston Symphony Orchestra chose
a native-born section principal for the first time in its history,
and by 1961 American singers were appearing with such
frequency at European opera houses that European unions
were grumbling about "Americanization."

The chief villain of the piece, those sitting around the
*Musical America*-AGMA table agreed, was the group attrac-

tion. Busloads of musicians and singers, traveling deep inland via superhighways, were usurping opportunities heretofore open to solo performers and chamber-music groups. The fee that groups asked collectively equaled the fee of a single great solo artist or string quartet. That was one reason local sponsors hastened to engage them. Another was that the huge new arts centers, theaters, gymnasiums and auditoriums in which they appeared everywhere in the country rendered the choice of large groups mandatory if an audience was going to be able to hear a performance. The solo performer was edged out because of these factors, and the law of supply and demand was working against artistic development.

All this, including the unbridled increase in number of group attractions, was hardly news to the participants at the conference. Eleven years before, *Musical America* advised editorially that "experience has shown that organized-audience committees are generally willing to risk engaging a group of performers none of whose names were [sic] previously known to them, whereas they typically put up stiff resistance to the proposal that they engage a soloist with whose name they are not familiar." On another page in the same issue, Kurt Weinhold of Columbia Artists said it was all the fault of the Korean War, rearmament, the cost of living and TV, which "accentuate a preference for ensemble attractions. It is a challenge to every manager to satisfy this popular demand without altering the basic cultural aspect of the concert field."

Unwilling to put the onus on sponsors or on social problems, Sol Hurok put the blame squarely on organized audience committees and New York managers in 1957. "Managers are not even selling high-class vaudeville, for there were once great people in vaudeville," he reminisced sadly in the *Los Angeles Times*. "It is harder to sell the single artist than it is to sell group attractions. So the philosophy prevails that if there are three people on the stage a concert is more important than if there is only one. . . ." Unable to tolerate this affront, Herbert O. Fox of Community hurriedly advised the

*Times* that "When I came into the concert business, very few groups were touring America, and almost all of them were managed by Sol Hurok. In the last few years he has doubled the proportion of groups on his list." From both offices have since flowed new and spectacular group attractions including military shows, puppet shows, Broadway shows and horse shows.

At the conference, both Hurok and Community were held to account. There was also general disapproval of sponsors who underestimated the musical tastes of their communities and were cultural dictators to boot. "Over and over again," wrote one participant afterwards, "one gets the impression that a large part of our country's musical life is in the hands of the wrong people, civic leaders with a terribly short-sighted idea of the nature of music." Even college and university concert managers, the white hope of the assembled savants, were not spared criticism. "All they want is jazz and hootenannies," wailed one manager who had none of either to offer.

A proposal that recitals be subsidized with foundation help drew approval—it neatly shifted the problem to other and sturdier shoulders—and there was general agreement that some sources outside the music field should underwrite such a project. But nobody could decide which source, which foundation, or how the project could get started. And during the next few years, while awaiting the results of an intensive and fruitful study by foundation scholars, the solo performer might very well have to investigate new paths of endeavor such as retraining programs.

In the opinions of some observers, the best solution was barely touched on at the conference, mainly because few managers would be willing to take responsibility for its success. That was to devise standards for both New York managers and local sponsors with respect to their choices of artists. Under these standards, the entire field could be operated more productively and efficiently. As long as sponsors and New York managers are willing to present and book the mediocre and the untalented en masse—in short, to operate strictly according to immediately profitable laws of supply and demand—budding solo talents will remain undeveloped and/or submerged in groups. Equally important, when the costs of a Town Hall or Carnegie Hall debut (which usually earns nothing at the box office) can take a large chunk of most people's life savings, many a talent, unfortunately with limited funds, cannot begin to compete and may be completely overlooked in the rush and the shouts of greedy and aggressive colleagues.

Of basic importance is the fact that Columbia and the Summy-Birchard Co. (which bought NCAC and Civic in 1961 from Luben Vichey) both dropped their New York recital divisions by 1963. These divisions presented aspiring performers regularly (at the prospective artist's own cost) and some effort was made in many cases to interest critics and artists' managers in attending, if the performers seemed to merit attention.

Perhaps the most important question in the music field today is whether the solo performer will go down the drain, deserted by critics, managers and public alike. There is a small if somewhat beleaguered band making efforts in his behalf, and hopefully this group of critics and managers can arouse an indifferent public, but the situation is not promising, and no great encouragement can (or should) be given to budding virtuosi.

In a celebrated inaugural address, President John F. Kennedy urged his countrymen to "Ask not what your country can do for you, ask what you can do for your country." The tragedy of the solo performer is that he is willing to give almost everything and is asked for nothing.

# VIII. *Spend Some*

"*When the Rockefeller brothers were children, their parents gave them small allowances. 'You've probably heard the stories,' John D. Rockefeller 3rd said the other day. 'We were given the money and told we should do three things with it—give some, save some . . .' He paused. 'Now what was the third thing?' he murmured. 'Oh,' he said, recalling, 'and we should spend some.'*"

—The New York Times, *December 7, 1967*

"*With but few exceptions the programs [of the Ford Foundation] under the Heald Regime were 'safe'; however useful, there was nothing daring or controversial in giving $80,200,000 to symphony orchestras.*"

—Fortune, *April 1968*

"*The symphony is good for Dallas. I'll be glad to do anything I can to help it, as long as you don't ask me to attend any concerts.*"

ROBERT L. THORNTON, *Founder,*
—*Citizens Council of Dallas*

## 1. *Why the square?*

AT 11:40 A.M. on May 14, 1959, President Dwight D. Eisenhower rose from his chair at ground-breaking ceremonies for Lincoln Center for the Performing Arts in New York City and told a crowd of 12,000 that a "mighty influence for peace and understanding throughout the world" was to be constructed on the site. The President also said that the center would symbolize American cultural independence and that it was a "stimulating approach" to urban blight. Then he dug up five shovelfuls of freshly turned earth with a chrome-plated shovel, one for the record and four for photographers.

Eisenhower, in a jovial mood, had earlier heard a musical program in which the performers were in a green-and-white tent. He drew some of the most appreciative laughter of the day when he asked "Of course, the performance does raise one question: If they can do this under a tent, why the square?"

The crowd was also in a good humor. Nobody was miffed by the question, and nobody pointed out that Leonard Bernstein, conductor of the New York Philharmonic and master of ceremonies, had already answered it, describing the center as a place where symphony, opera, the dance, repertory theater, museums and schools would be nurtured. The following day, Howard Taubman of *The New York Times* described the center for the benefit of readers as "much more than a monument to American impatience with the old." Taubman anticipated "a complex of new buildings in which established as well as fresh institutions will dedicate themselves to serving music, theatre and dance so as to meet the needs of a democracy in the second half of the twentieth century."

Taubman's article appeared under the headline "Lincoln Center will fulfill a great need, but is faced by many problems." Few problems were cited, but the guests of honor at the ceremonies included some of New York's top-level businessmen and philanthropists, and there was confidence that they would find solutions if problems did come up. Chief among them was John D. Rockefeller III, chairman of the Rockefeller Foundation, a trustee of the Rockefeller Brothers Fund and a third-generation member of a family whose name was synonomous with great wealth. Also present was Robert Moses, builder of roadways and world's fairs, adviser to presidents, high-level civil servant with a reputation for getting things done.

Moses had actually started the Lincoln Center project off in 1954, when the Metropolitan Opera was interested in building a new house within the New York Coliseum complex. As Parks Commissioner, Moses vetoed the idea because it seemed impossible to slip the privileged and exclusive Metropolitan into a building put up with public funds. At about the same time Robert Simon, who owned Carnegie Hall, announced that the hall would be sold and then probably demolished. This would dispossess the Philharmonic Orchestra. Anthony Bliss, president of the Metropolitan, met with a Philharmonic board member and then with Rockefeller to find a way to make common cause for new and possibly joint facilities.

Robert Moses then stepped back into the story by suggesting that an urban-renewal project at Lincoln Square on the West Side of Manhattan could be a site for buildings devoted to the arts. He is also reputed to have suggested the original group of Lincoln Center constituents—Fordham's Law School, the Metropolitan, the Philharmonic, the Juilliard School of Music and Title I housing.

Rockefeller has set the time of his earliest involvement with the center in September 1955. While attending a conference of the Council on Foreign Relations in Pennsylvania's Pocono Mountains, he met with Charles Spofford, a lawyer and past president and active member of the Metropolitan Opera Association. Seated on a park bench, the two men began talking about the state of the arts in America. Spofford volunteered that the Metropolitan Opera had been offered "a last-chance opportunity" to acquire land for a new home and that the New York Philharmonic's chairman, Arthur Houghton, Jr., had recently visited architect Wallace Harrison to discuss the design of a new home for the orchestra, "nothing too ambitious, not for a corner plot, just a single façade."

These "three coincidences"—the Metropolitan's decision to move, the Philharmonic's need for a new home and the availability of land in Lincoln Square—set Rockefeller to thinking. "It was," he later reminisced, "a fascinating set of circumstances." He promptly joined Spofford's Exploratory Committee for a Musical Arts Center, which was to meet every two weeks for lunch at New York's Century Club.

Events then began to move swiftly. In October, Rockefeller was chairman of the committee and deep in organizational plans. He met with the Philadelphia firm of Day and Zimmerman, consulting and management engineers, who prepared a feasibility study, estimating construction costs for the center at $55 million. To this, the committee added $20 million for contingencies and to establish a fund for "educational, creative, and artistic advancement."

Nothing like $75 million had ever been raised before in the course of a single campaign for the arts, but Rockefeller and the committee believed it could be done, and independently of any government help that might be obtained. To prove it, one of the most prestigious businessmen in the country, Clarence Francis, former chairman of the General Foods Corporation, was recruited as campaign chairman. He in turn began organizing a committee of volunteer fund raisers consisting of some of the leading bankers, lawyers and businessmen in the city.

In the early spring of 1956, Rockefeller set forth for Europe with a Day and Zimmerman staff member, Harrison and Bliss. They observed "artistic and educational institutions in London, Paris, Vienna, Milan, Strasbourg, and Cologne." They also spread news about their embryonic plans. One of the best responses was heard in Milan, where the director of La Scala said, "Up to now, music has had two capitals: Milan and New York. After your center is built there will be only one—New York."

All this was very encouraging to Rockefeller, and the final decision that "a performing arts center was feasible and desirable" was made when he returned to New York. In June 1956 Lincoln Center for the Performing Arts was incorporated as a nonprofit membership organization, the members of the Exploratory Committee becoming directors of the center.

The new directors promptly decided that the center would consist of a group of six institutions—the Metropolitan Opera, the New York Philharmonic, the Juilliard School of Music, the New York City Center, a library-museum of the performing arts and a theatrical repertory company—each to retain artistic and fiscal autonomy. Each institution would be represented on the board of directors of Lincoln Center; its "chief professional officer" would serve with his peers at these institutions on the Lincoln Center Council. The board of directors would also include "distinguished men of achievement in business and the professions . . . devoted to the Lincoln Center idea," as well as the Mayor of the City of New York and the Commissioner of Parks as ex officio members.

The first overall commander chosen for the enterprise was Major General Maxwell Taylor, World War II leader of the 101st Airborne, the "Screaming Eagles." Taylor was appointed president in January 1961. This choice was thought odd in the music world, but Taylor soon resigned to become President Kennedy's military adviser. The position was taken by William Schuman, president of the Juilliard School of Music and a noted composer, on January 1, 1962.

In the fall of 1959, clearance of the construction site was begun, and a group of renowned architects and planners from the United States and abroad was assembled "to advise on the overall site plan and on general architectural considerations." The "design objective" they were given "was to provide, for each of the arts, a place of performance as close to ideal as economics would permit." By "ideal" Rockefeller partly meant "buildings to stand for 100 years." He bade everyone at Lincoln Center commit himself "to standards of quality."

It is said by Rockefeller that "numerous working models were created and, one by one, criticized, altered and discarded." Other sources disclose that there was no consensus for an overall master plan and that the assembled savants bogged down in petty rivalries. Rockefeller was asked to join discussions and become a "guide, philosopher and friend," but it was Robert Moses who brought order out of the confusion among such giants of the architectural establishment as Wallace Harrison, Eero Saarinen, Max Abramovitz, Philip Johnson, Pietro Belluschi and Gordon Bunshaft.

Moses simply fixed the boundaries of his own pet project, Damrosch Park, the center's site for band concerts. He thus determined the western boundary of the New York State

Theater (to house the New York City Center) and the southern boundary of the Metropolitan Opera. From that point, each architect was free to develop plans within his own fief.

Five buildings with white travertine exteriors (the Italian stone of which the Colosseum is made) were envisioned. These, plus the park and the bandstand, were to be grouped around a plaza as big as the Piazza San Marco in Venice. Dominating the fourteen-acre center would be the Metropolitan Opera House. Off to the north, across the plaza, came the Juilliard School. East of the plaza came Philharmonic Hall, new home for the New York Philharmonic. Facing Philharmonic Hall was to be a matched building, the State Theater. Yet another massive structure was planned to house the repertory theater and the library-museum.

It is doubtful whether the builders of the Louvre, the Acropolis or St. Peter's launched forth with such enthusiasm as did the creators of Lincoln Center. Press releases continually alerted the masses to the great things in prospect. "Future generations of visitors from America and abroad will come to Lincoln Center as they now visit great landmarks in Venice, Athens and Rome, just for the joy of being there," said one brochure. "Lincoln Center will make New Yorkers proud. It will make America proud."

But there were those in 1956 who already found it a mixed blessing.

First were 1,647 families in the renewal area with no place to go when their 188 tenements were torn down. They saw the center less as a cultural adventure than as yet another intrusion by the rich into the limited living space in Manhattan. It was not until the fall of 1959 that they were all relocated, at the center's expense, to better apartments. Lincoln Center was hailed a great success if only as a real-estate project.

Then there was the rescue of Carnegie Hall in 1960, an event that seemingly lessened the need for Philharmonic Hall.

It developed, however, that the rescuers had no explicit purpose in saving the hall other than that it was a historical landmark. While they pondered this dilemma and busily got public funds to pay for the acquisition, the spotlight swung back to Lincoln Center.

Here relationships between some of the constituent groups came under discussion. Each member organization, said Lincoln Center, was to be master in its own house. But according to an official brochure, "The whole is greater than the sum of its parts," and the constituents would seek for "common artistic goals." Who would define these common goals? And once defined, who would pursue their achievement? Was New York's cultural life to be enriched or was it to be merely ornamented?

## 2. *An ever-expanding force*

Against such a background, the press constantly sought details of policy, program and architectural plans from center executives. William F. Powers, executive director of construction, was asked how many tons of concrete would go into the project, how many miles of pipe and wire, how many steel beams.

Powers was hurt by the question. Steel and concrete, he pointed out, could be measured.

"However," he added disarmingly, "such an image would fall far short of the *real* description of Lincoln Center. Far better would be some measure of the more intangible ingredients which will be combined and distributed to produce for the public the cultural benefits of this undertaking. The new results will not be measured in terms of buildings and halls, steel and concrete, or pipe and wire; but rather in the influence on the cultural, recreational and mental aspects of life in New York for residents and visitors from every corner of the globe."

A fondness for this type of poetic flight came to characterize the public statements of the architects, urban planners, engineers, draftsmen, musicians, philanthropists, businessmen, fund raisers, lawyers, bankers, builders, educators, acousticians and politicians who pooled their abilities to labor for the center's betterment and development. All felt the eyes of future generations upon them. The larger concept, the utopia to be created—not the petty detail—came to occupy their thoughts.

On the other hand, bills had a tendency to come due in the present, and there were understandable pleas to the public to support efforts with financial gifts. It was further determined that some cultural activities were going to cost customers more than they had in less fancy surroundings.

Thus the February 8, 1962, *New York Times* bore news that tickets for the Boston Symphony Orchestra's 1962–63 series at Philharmonic Hall would average 50 percent higher than tickets for its 1961–62 series at Carnegie Hall, with the largest percentage of increase being in the lowest priced seats. One explanation for this inflationary wave was that Philharmonic Hall's rental fees were going to be higher than Carnegie Hall's.

Those depressed by such tidings could take heart in progress reports on the center's fund-raising campaign. Between 1955 and 1963 the announced goal was to rise from $75 million to $160.7 million, but victory shouts were heard as early as May 7, 1962, when a *Times* headline said "Lincoln Center will start drive for last $28 million"—and the goal was $142 million. The story quoted Edward Young, the center's executive vice president, as saying that fund raising was actually helping to reduce ticket prices.

"We want to complete the job without having to borrow a nickel," Mr. Young explained. "If we have to borrow it would put the public at a disadvantage, because the interest that would have to be paid on the loan would have to be met by charging higher seat prices." As an example, Young pointed out that if the $4 million needed to complete Philharmonic Hall was borrowed the 5 percent interest on the loan would amount to $200,000, and this would result in the public's paying at least twenty-five cents extra for each seat.

To complete construction, a "relentless, year-long" fund campaign was to be announced at the annual meeting of the center's board of directors the same month. The national and international significance of the project was further stressed. However, a soupçon of doubt had also crept in. "Every fund-raising campaign starts enthusiastically with large gifts and then reaches a point where activity begins to slow down," Young observed. "Since we recently reached this leveling plateau, we decided to plan a last, all-out push to the top of the mountain."

In June, the *Times* carried heartening news that the New York City Planning Commission had approved an allocation of $4.3 million in capital funds as the city's site-acquisition share of the $20.4 million New York State Theater Building (for which the state had also provided $15 million). But in November, Federal Government accountants in Washington were questioning a $2.7 million grant-in-aid credit by the Urban Renewal Administration for the plaza. The administration manfully stood its ground, declaring that "although the Plaza will be physically located in the [Lincoln Center] area, it will serve the entire city, as well as tourists visiting the city."

On April 15, 1963, the Ford Foundation made its largest single grant yet to an arts project—$12.5 million—to Lincoln Center. The second paragraph of the *Times* story reporting the gift noted, however, that costs had somehow run away again, and the center was shorter—by $2.5 million—of its fund-raising goal than it had been the year before. "A recent review of present and projected costs for center structures" disclosed that the budget had climbed to $160.7 million. This was $85.7 million more than the 1955 goal and $18.7 million more than the 1962 goal.

Eight days later Rockefeller announced an additional Rockefeller Foundation gift of $5 million, which helped, but the Ford Foundation was clearly growing weary of the burden and said that its recent $12.5 million gift would be the final one "in this decade." Thus far $40 million had come from Federal, state and city governments. Of the remaining $100 million in donations, more than half represented contributions by the Ford and Rockefeller Foundations and the Rockefeller family.

In September, "the top of the mountain" seemed nearer—Lincoln Center needed only $19.3 million—and the first annual report showed that $1.6 million had been spent on fund raising. This represented only 1.6 percent of the amount received (in nongovernmental gifts) and was considered an extremely low sum, relatively. The report also described a limited program of guided tours that was to be offered on an experimental basis. Visitors could get a 45-minute trip around the center for a modest charge of only 60 cents per person.

By mid-1964 the drive was growing somewhat less relentless, and Rockefeller was offering to raise up to $8 million more himself to complete the campaign, which had raised a grand total of $145.6 million. Rockefeller volunteered to match "on a dollar for dollar basis what others can obtain and give before the end of 1964." Others gave only $5.8 million more by November; however, costs went up, and the center was still short $10.9 million of its goal. It looked as if his offer might have to be extended into 1965.

"Lincoln Center gets $1.1 million; Clarks' gift brings drive to $4.5 million of goal," reported the *Times* on July 6, 1965, but it was January 30, 1966, before the drive was officially declared completed, and, as a matter of fact, had gone $4.7 million over the goal.

Alas, paragraph two of the *Times* story announcing the success also said that "unforeseen expenses incurred since 1963" had absorbed the overage, and $1.4 million was still needed to complete the Juilliard School. Indeed there had been some miscalculations. Philharmonic Hall had cost 250 percent more than budgeted, the Metropolitan and the Beaumont Theater 100 percent more. The New York State Theater was estimated at $17 million but cost $25 million.

The total cost of the center ($166.8 million in 1966) now represented one of the largest fund campaigns in American history in any field. "The Lincoln Center campaign has given the arts a place in philanthropy that they have never enjoyed before," thought William Schuman. "The size of the objective and the fact that it was being sought for the arts, which had never before received wide philanthropic support, make this effort a milestone, one whose achievement should stimulate and inspire others," predicted Clarence Francis.

Easily the most inspired were Lincoln Center directors, who announced in December 1967 yet another fund campaign that they hoped would raise $3 million a year to support the Lincoln Center Fund. (Its purpose was to make the center "an ever-expanding force in providing continuing support for its artistic and educational programs.") The fund had already received $11.9 million through 1967—surpassing its own goal of $10 million. This new drive was in addition to annual maintenance drives by the Metropolitan Opera, the Philharmonic and other constituents, which needed between $12 million and $15 million per year.

Then there was the matter of another $9 million that the center said was still needed for odds and ends of construction. "Our business is to lose money wisely," Schuman advised, but he had to admit there were those inside and outside the center family who were objecting to the center's proliferation into more and more areas, including films. "There is money to support these things and support them handsomely," Schuman said. "The sources of support are just beginning to be tapped."

## 3. *The validity of our efforts*

The white-tie premiere concert in Philharmonic Hall, the first Lincoln Center building to be opened, was given on

September 23, 1962, and had Mrs. John F. Kennedy, the President's wife, at the head of the guest list. Tickets were priced from $100 to $250 ($250,000 was raised), and so fashionable was the event that even police were dressed in tuxedos. The demand for chauffeur-driven limousines far exceeded the supply. Major rental agencies were forced to bring up luxury cars from as far as Philadelphia and New Haven.

Despite a heroic last-minute attempt to complete the hall on schedule, much remained to be done. Foyers and promenades looked shiny, but anyone wearing white kid gloves soiled them on undusted banisters. The outdoor terrace commanded an imposing view of the city, but access was barred by two-by-fours. Richard Lippold's highly-touted five-ton sculpture "Orpheus and Apollo" was missing three-quarters of its several hundred gold metal sheets. Odd corners were unpainted; gold-jacketed bartenders downstairs in the café apologized because Philharmonic Hall matchbooks had not yet arrived.

Complicating last-minute preparations was the fact that the concert was also a television show on a coast-to-coast network, and workmen had been setting up equipment since 6 A.M. Rockefeller appeared early in the show to deliver the welcoming address. "This is a proud and happy moment for all of us," he said. "Now and in the years ahead, only the artist and his art can fulfill the aspirations of the planners and exalt the labors of the builders. The validity of our efforts will be determined by the use we make of the several stages and many classrooms of Lincoln Center, and it is gratifying indeed that we have as our president a distinguished composer and educator."

The program, under Leonard Bernstein's direction, had as participants the Philharmonic, thirteen vocal soloists and three choruses and, as a major feature, a new work by Aaron Copland. This was one occasion when the music was less important than the location, however, and the audience, which included many prominent musicians, devoted itself to a reconnaissance of the hall, with special attention to its acoustics.

One woman told a friend, "I couldn't imagine how it was going to look. It was so ugly for so long." Many praised its modernity and décor. Next morning some members of the press still thought it was pretty ugly, however. Winthrop Sargeant of *The New Yorker* detected an "Alcatraz motif": "The views of Mr. Abramovitz's edifice from the Broadway and Sixty-fifth street sides strongly suggest a very modern escape-proof cell block, with tier upon tier of glassed-in walks." Harold Schonberg of the *Times* was scarcely more encouraging about acoustics. "From Row R on the orchestra floor the sound was clear, a little dry, with not much reverberation and a decided lack of bass."

Schonberg did, however, hold out hope for the hall. "On the basis of present accomplishment, Philharmonic Hall should turn out to be a fine theater in the modern style: not a mellow house but a clear, uncolored, vigorous one, in which each strand of musical material will be easily followed." Such was also the thinking of Virgil Thomson, Samuel Barber and Rosina Lhevinne.

To offset any anger that guests felt about construction in the area, the souvenir program included an insertion by Young, listing the "unfinished situations" that might lead to congestion and inconveniences. As the audience left, many persons also found free champagne had been set up on tables in the various foyers. Thirsty and uncomplaining first-nighters filled glasses and drank toasts to the center.

But Lincoln Center was soon the focus of unseemly and unartistic discord over Philharmonic Hall's acoustics. Leo Beranek, the acoustical engineer who had measured and evaluated fifty-four concert halls and opera houses in Europe, Israel and the Americas to find the secret of good acoustics, admitted that the bass sound in the auditorium had to be "reinforced." A committee of four acoustical experts recruited by William Schuman said that the hall suffered from "severe acoustic limitations" but, fortunately, "the basic shape of the auditorium is good." Beranek refused to comment on

the findings of the consultant acousticians, the Philadelphia
Orchestra debated returning to Carnegie Hall for its annual
New York series and Schuman pointed out to the press that
it was "no secret" that the hall had "certain deficiencies."

The failure was considered so monumental that up to 1969
more than $1.5 million would be spent to correct faults.
Philharmonic officials (the orchestra's, not the hall's) managed
to hide their hurt from the press. In private (as to the present
writer) they disclaimed any responsibility for construction,
neatly shifting the burden to Abramovitz and Beranek. On
the other hand they were obligated to pay most of the
$750,000 bill in a last-ditch effort to subdue the hall's echo.

Not so discreet were other actual and prospective Lincoln
Center constituents. It began to leak to the newspapers that
all was not well at council meetings. Constituents often criticized each other unmercifully. Disillusionment began to set
in with the realization that the men in charge represented
a sort of cultural old guard, interested more in status and
show than in artistic and cultural innovation.

The internal dissension was best illustrated by the jockeying
for power among constituents. At first the Byzantine politics
were treated by the center's officials as growing pains. Then
an unseemly struggle between William Schuman and Rudolph
Bing, general manager of the Metropolitan, over one Herman
Krawitz, an assistant manager of the Metropolitan, came to
light.

At issue was not only Krawitz but the operations of
the Vivian Beaumont Theater and the Lincoln Center Repertory Company, and the continued residency of its managing
producer, Robert Whitehead. To use the phrase of an earlier
strategist, Schuman probed the soft underbelly of both the
Met and the repertory theater by trying to hire Krawitz
away from Bing to take Whitehead's place.

The repercussions were immediate. Bing threatened to resign
from the Lincoln Center Council and issued a violent protest
declaring that the center was "apparently deteriorating into

a free-for-all jungle whose constituents can raid each other at will." Anthony Bliss said flatly that Krawitz would not be released. Whitehead announced that he could no longer work with Schuman and also said, "I do not think [William Schuman] is a constructive force." Robert Hoguet, Jr., president of the repertory theater, asserted that the theater "still hoped to prevail on the Met Board to let Krawitz go." Arthur Miller, the playwright, threatened to take his plays elsewhere. Schuman was unavailable for comment to the press for a two-week period.

As yet, there was no center supreme court for the adjudication of quarrels, but Rockefeller took a "relaxed view" of developments, and Schuman's position was said to be secure. In further developments, Whitehead resigned but Krawitz remained at the Metropolitan and Bing remained at Lincoln Center.

Soon afterward Schuman took on Morton Baum, president of the City Center. At issue this time was the New York State Theater. Baum insisted that the house had been created for the City Center and that it was an autonomous unit. Not so, said Schuman. He insisted that Lincoln Center retained "responsibility for the Theater including the right to book it when the City Center was not using it."

Morton Baum was a sensitive man, a man of culture, a chess player, a pianist, an omnivorous reader. Morton Baum was also a rough, tough and competitive lawyer and businessman. At the City Center he had stepped on the toes of press, Wall Street bigwigs and society figures alike. Nor was he a novice at administration. Baum had taken care of bookings, budgets, finances and fights with City Hall, for which he had a special aptitude.

In short, he was well equipped for life at Lincoln Center, but it was thought a hopeless struggle—David versus Goliath. How could Baum and the City Center fight Schuman and Lincoln Center? Yet it soon developed that the odds were all on Baum's side. An infighter, he used legalistic tricks not known before at Lincoln Center. He confused, outraged, frightened his opponents. One shocking request was that all books of Lincoln Center constituents be examined to determine operating efficiency.

When the controversy ended, the City Center was in control of its own operations at the State Theater and Baum was in control of the City Center. Schuman and the Lincoln Center board were somewhat shaken.

If Lincoln Center's internal squabbles had been attributable merely to the wrong men in the right positions or to growing pains, all the quarrels would have had limited relevance to culture in America. But a wider understanding was becoming prevalent. A solid financing operation, a brilliant building enterprise and a successful slum-clearance project had checked the course of urban decay in a West Side area that was rapidly going downhill. But what had been done to the bright, idealistic dreams for culture?

Hopefully, three years of efforts since the opening of Philharmonic Hall would not forecast an eternity of disharmony, but some of the reasons for the sorry state seemed to be built into the enterprise. No structure or program was going to be the free, dedicated, uncompromised work of one or two individuals. "Committees" composed of board members would be operative everywhere. And, as in all such situations, the results would not really be bad and not really be good. Mostly they would be middlebrow and mediocre, with considerable time spent calming nerves and soothing tempers.

Equally bad, the troubles that swirled around Lincoln Center had come near to discrediting both the idea of a publicly supported culture and the intentions of the business community that had taken leadership. "America needs a repertory theater," Harold Clurman told *Newsweek*. "But it won't be given to us by businessmen." "We leave important public activities to be privately supported," wrote Benjamin

Boretz of the *Nation*. "And thus, also to be governed almost entirely by the whim of the privately moneyed, regardless of public interest or professional need."

## 4. *Throw him out*

The romance between big money and culture was off to a shaky start at Lincoln Center. It began to make real headway, however, when the Ford Foundation, the richest philanthropic organization in the world, began lavishing gifts on the performing arts in 1962.

Like their counterparts at Lincoln Center, Ford Foundation trustees were a prestigious group of business and civic leaders. In 1962, they included Benson Ford, Henry Ford II, two educators, one Federal judge, one banker, one business executive, two corporation lawyers, three publishing magnates, two manufacturers and President Henry Heald, former president of New York University. A firm, draconian approach to largesse was espoused. "Of course, you can't expect philanthropy to run precisely like a business," Heald once said, "but we do take a hard look at each proposal before we invest, to make sure our money will produce social returns—in other words, earn a fair 'nonprofit.' "

Nonetheless a basic problem at the foundation was that for reasons of financial control of the Ford Motor Company by the Ford family, and to preserve the legal tax-deductible status of the foundation, money could not be allowed to accumulate in the treasury. Trustees were sometimes faced with the necessity to disgorge huge amounts quickly. So well did they do in this direction that in its first twelve years of existence, Ford gave away $1.7 billion in grants. This accounted for all the income on capital and $525 million of the capital itself. Almost half the money went to educational institutions.

The arts were not among the foundation's major interests

until 1957, when a modest grant was made to assist the development of "creative persons" and to "explore the relationship [between] the artist, his institutions and the public." Between $2 million and $3 million was thereupon appropriated each year under a program titled "Humanities and the Arts." Poets in San Francisco, pianists in New York and playwrights in Houston were among the foundation's first beneficiaries.

The program soon accounted for half the mail received by the foundation. Announcements of grants made clear, however, that the money was being given not simply so that some wretch could write or perform, but so that some higher artistic or national purpose could be served. This was in keeping with the foundation's policy in other fields, where every project had to have a bearing on a problem.

W. McNeil Lowry, first director of the Humanities and Arts program, provided some thoughts on the training of artists in America in 1962. Lowry advised university deans not to educate painters and sculptors in the way they were doing it. "Under present conditions the best service you can perform for the potential artist is to throw him out," he wrote in the *Educational Theatre Journal*.

The statement was not so lamentable as a startled reader might first suppose. What Lowry went on to say was that the universities were duty bound to produce artists with professional standards, if they were going to offer professional degrees. They were also duty bound to produce audiences with some degree of taste and discrimination if they were going to offer courses in appreciation. "The future of professional training in the arts depends," said Lowry, "first, upon a radical shift in the university atmosphere surrounding students considered potential artists, and, second, upon the provision of opportunities for professional apprenticeship through non-academic persons or institutions."

These good definitive statements spoke well for Lowry's prospective administration of the program. An attitude insistent on high standards evidently informed the approval of grants. Furthermore, Lowry was by reputation a man who spoke his mind, unafraid of trustees or foundation brass. He had never done much in the arts himself, but as one future grantee was to say, "He's always interested in the creative qualities of people. When he meets people in the creative fields he meets them on a sympathetic basis."

Except for Lincoln Center, no spectacular grants followed announcement of the Humanities and Arts program. Foundation trustees considered the results of the experimental program successful and encouraging, and Lowry went on record as preferring not to discuss matters of style, form and subject in connection with gifts to the arts. "Ford," said Lowry, "tries not to influence this situation"—meaning artistic movements. In the music field, many shook their heads in disbelief. By simply making a grant, the foundation was making a value judgment, one that might prove disastrous to a beneficiary's competitors. How could matters of style, form and content go undiscussed? On what basis, then, was a grant made?

Meanwhile, foundation trustees, hard at work on the nation's problems, came to the belief that the Federal government was not likely to sponsor a major subsidy program in the arts, owing to budgetary priorities for national security. "Foreign leaders" also told them that "one of the greatest services they could perform internationally would be to strengthen the quality and fabric of American society at home." One way to accomplish this was the encouragement of the creative and performing arts, and on July 1, 1962, a Ford statement of plans called for both a continued international program and emphasis on "the problems and needs of the United States."

Like Lincoln Center, the foundation was not given to modest goals (or modest announcements), and when its plan was unveiled, there were those who detected a certain expansiveness and lack of overall purpose. The *Times* asked, "Is the foundation not still trying to embrace too many activities in too many fields, with consequent dilution of its potential effectiveness? Even the relatively large resources of the Ford Foundation are dwarfed by the immensity of the needs existing here and abroad."

Lowry, in turn, emphasized that support would be possible for only a fraction of the activities proposed, at least in the arts field. "The sky is not the limit," he said. He also added a new philosophical note: "Art has much to do with the drive or fanaticism of the person who has made his choice and will eschew anything else—money, the elite identification of a degree, even health—to develop the talent he has." Lowry was also discovering that some of the most talented and mature artists somehow lacked "either the time or capacity to sort out a decent personal life." Unhappily, "only a rare heredity or early environment and not—probably—a very good education has given some of these artists a humanity that separates them from the talented bums in their midst."

Evidently these were not snap judgments but the results of interviews with hundreds of artists and personal visits to some fifty communities around the country. Lowry and his staff had attempted to keep in touch with every important cultural trend. In New York there was a constant stream of experts into and out of the Ford Foundation office at 477 Madison Avenue.

In October 1963, came the first major results of this study with gifts of $1.7 million to thirteen opera companies to help them expand their activities. A short time before, $950,-000 was given to the big four in opera—the Metropolitan, the New York City, the Chicago Lyric, and the San Francisco—to produce up to eighteen operas written by Americans. "Professional opera is everywhere a deficit operation," confided Lowry to the press. This was not exactly news, but he hoped that the gifts would allow companies to increase their local support and to produce some new operas.

The outcome was to be otherwise. Within a few years, the Chicago Lyric Opera was temporarily out of business and the Metropolitan had been forced to drop its national touring company; audiences were generally bored and unimpressed by the commissions. Few new works were thought good enough to be performed a second time.

New phalanxes of experts were needed. A new term was coined—"Foundation music"—to describe those unique works by which no audiences felt benefited, stimulated or emotionally affected, but which had been brought into existence by the students and friends of renowned experts.

Lowry and his staff were also busy in the ballet field, where "the standards of instruction are dangerously low" and few companies had "any sort of artistic and financial stability." In December 1963, $7.7 million went to eight organizations to further development of professional ballet. This was the largest sum any foundation had ever allotted to one performing art at one time. Moreover, of the total amount, $5.9 million went to two affiliated institutions in New York, the New York City Ballet and the School of American Ballet, both headed by George Balanchine and Lincoln Kirstein.

"The facts of the dance world in this country as they existed last Sunday [December 15] are no more, and they will never ever be the same," cried the *Times*. "The Ford Foundation has declared by the bestowal of nearly $6 million that the dance technique and style preferred by George Balanchine are so superior to any others existing in this country that they should be developed to the virtual exclusion of all others." The article also charged that if the foundation had consciously intended to set up a monopoly for Balanchine it could not have done so in a better way.

There were those in the modern dance world who are said to have nearly lost their reason on hearing news of the grant. More than a month later, cries of protest were still heard from Martha Graham, José Limon, Ruth St. Denis and Ted Shawn. Sinister connotations were drawn from the fact that several grantees within the program were former dis-

ciples of Balanchine. One shocker was the grant of $295,000
to a dance troupe in Wilkes-Barre, which was a bare five
and a half months old. "It is strange," wrote Allen Hughes
in the *Times*, "until you understand that George Balanchine
and Lincoln Kirstein think there should be a Pennsylvania
Ballet . . . that Mrs. [Barbara] Weisberger should head it,
and that the Ford Foundation should contribute to its establishment."

Lowry was accused of naïveté in his concentration on
Balanchine but assured critics that modern dance would not
be ignored in the future. (And it was not. In August 1968,
seven groups shared $485,000.) But at the moment he was
hard pressed to think of when and how, since the multi-
million-dollar grant represented the Ford Foundation's long-
range contribution to the dance. Happily some support came
from John Martin in the *Saturday Review*, who thought the
most regrettable thing was not the grant but the press release
that announced it—"conventionally foundationese in style, it
was almost clinical in content, stating all the facts with un-
disputable clarity but ignoring the realities that animated
them."

In subsequent developments the New York City Opera
was given $250,000 to put on a season of contemporary opera.
Lowry was promoted to vice president in charge of policy and
planning. Under his administration general arts project grants
totaling $43.6 million had been made. Succeeding him as
director of the Humanities and Arts program was Sigmund
Koch, a former professor of psychology at Duke University.

Lowry's elevation was not a promotion upstairs to obscurity, but the signal for increased aid to the arts at Ford.
In October 1965 came a blockbuster announcement—$85
million for about fifty symphony orchestras throughout the
country. Nearly eleven times greater than the ballet grants, it
was the largest sum ever allocated at one fell swoop to the arts.
With fifty involved, nobody could complain about favoritism.
Eight years in the preparation, the grant drew widespread en-

thusiasm from the music world. "A long awaited event of incalculable importance has finally taken place," Leonard Bernstein said, but he warned the public "not to sit back and relax in [its] support." Dr. Koch also issued a statement explaining why the foundation was aiding orchestras rather than other arts organizations. It was, he said, because they were more "mature organizations," established landmarks on the American scene.

Yet even this display of largesse was destined to be criticized. Expenditures by American orchestras were expected to reach $57.1 million by 1975. The income from the gift would hardly be more than 10 percent of that figure. Moreover, only $21 million was to be granted on a nonmatching basis—$64 million would have to be matched in ratios of one to one or two to one by each orchestra.

It was July 1966, before the recipients were chosen, and by that time the number of orchestras that would share had risen to sixty-one (more than two hundred applied), but the amount to be shared had gone down $4.8 million, to $80.2 million. The nation's twenty-five major orchestras (those with annual budgets exceeding $250,000) were included, as well as thirty-six smaller orchestras, virtually all with budgets over $100,000.

Two years later, a *Times* story titled "Nation's Orchestras Unsettled by Need to Match Ford Grants," found that only nine of the sixty-one orchestras had reached their goals. At least ten other ensembles were halfway or more to the finish line, which had to be reached by the close of the five-year Ford program on June 30, 1971, if the orchestras receiving matching gifts were to qualify. Some managers feared the demise of their organizations if fund drives failed. "The Ford grant has become the Good Housekeeping Seal of Approval," said one symphony orchestra manager. "We'll get the money, by hook or by crook, because we must."

Ford largesse was having the disquieting result of spreading a mild panic among orchestras, somewhat similar to salesmen's contests. There was a scramble for donors. Nor was confidence bolstered by word that McGeorge Bundy, president of the foundation, was privately expressing concern that theater companies, which had earlier received grants, were too "dependent" on the foundation for financial assistance. Should the theater groups continue to count on the "Lowry dowry," wondered Bundy? Probably not, despite the fact that it was difficult to withdraw from a project and publicly admit failure when it backfired.

On assuming the presidency, Bundy had promised the public "to put our money where our mouth is" and to give a hand to "those who are academically unfashionable, or unpleasing to orthodox intellectuals." He was on the lookout for ways to prod, push, persuade. The arts field was one area that needed as much help as it could get. And yet, Ford was still not sure of its responsibilities or the effects of its grants after $183.6 million allotted to the arts, and years of study.

## 5. *The best tribute*

1962 may well go down as the great watershed year in American cultural history. Lincoln Center opened Philharmonic Hall, the Ford Foundation launched into the arts and John F. Kennedy unveiled the cultural look on the New Frontier, an event greeted with great approval. The President's initial move was to appoint August Heckscher, a writer and foundation director, to a part-time post. Heckscher's job was to be "cultural coordinator" between the President and various governmental and private agencies. A little more than a year later Heckscher resigned—not as a protest against governmental policies, he said, but because he had originally agreed to serve only six months.

"Dear Augie," President Kennedy wrote back, "The best tribute to the success of your work is the decision to establish this function on a full-time and, I hope, permanent basis."

This was encouraging, but Heckscher left behind an eighty-page report sweepingly critical of the government's attitude toward the arts, hinting at adverse government influences and at agencies working at cross-purposes. A major failing, he asserted, was the absence of any coherent policy. Heckscher urged that Washington's National Cultural Center, then in the planning stage, serve as an example to other cities in providing wide cultural opportunities.

Before much coordination could be done, however, the New Frontier and Lincoln Center had sparked such a cultural building boom as delighted the construction industry and overwhelmed music lovers accustomed to performances in high school auditoriums. By July 1962 some form of building connected with the arts was planned or underway in sixty-nine cities, involving $375 million of public and private funds. Arts centers ranged from Lincoln Center in New York to a $10,000 building in Key West. Arts centers were created in an old canning factory in Yakima, a pumping station in Statesville, North Carolina, and a city jail in Tacoma. Thirteen states either set up arts councils or planned to establish them. In New York City, an impassioned resident of Queens wrote the *Times* that the borough was a "cultural desert," despite its proximity to Lincoln Center. He called for the preservation of the Music Hall at the World's Fair for a Queens arts center.

Prodigies of cultural fund raising were accomplished. Dorothy Buffum Chandler single-handedly asked for and got $18.5 million to construct the Music Center in Los Angeles. Not content, she then organized a company to float $13.7 million in bonds to finish the job. Dr. George Henry Alexander Clowes of Indianapolis decried art in large cities. "It is," said Dr. Clowes, "the smaller cities of America which have the opportunity afforded by singleness of purpose and selection, to form a civic personality which the babel of metropolitan centers makes impossible." He then gave $2.3 million of the $3.5 million needed for Clowes Memorial Hall.

A San Franciscan named Robert Hornby proposed a bond

issue of $29 million for a cultural center "that will be the envy of every city in the world." Less sanguinary citizens voted it down more than two to one. Hornby deplored the defeat, not only as a blow against culture but because of the "damage to the economy of the city in the form of jobs and income, from the cabby and waiter to stagehands and artists."

Interest in culture, said researchers in the field, was the newest status symbol. 1964 was to see a $3 billion market including everything from Plato to Puccini. This did not represent the expected peak. Experts predicted that the $3 billion market would double itself by 1970. Encouragement stemmed from information that between 1953 and 1960 spending on the arts had risen by about 130 percent. Support for worthy projects seemed everywhere assured; the state of New Jersey announced that an arts center abutting the Garden State Parkway at Telegraph Hill would be supported entirely by road tolls.

But in the midst of all this good news came a report that staggered cultural pioneers with its pessimism. In 1966, the Twentieth Century Fund's *Performing Arts: The Economic Dilemma* indicated that buildings might be going up but performing artists were still having a pretty dreary time of it. The financial state of the theater, the opera, the symphony, the dance and other interpretive arts was described as deplorable. In rich America, while centers were opened, the most significant artistic issue was who was going to make up a growing income gap between what came in at the box office and what it actually cost to maintain a dance troupe, an opera company or a symphony orchestra.

Moreover, there was an emerging suspicion that many an arts center had nothing of value to present. The words of R. Philip Hanes, Jr., president of the National Arts Councils of America, are illustrative. "Everybody wants to build a cultural center," observed Mr. Hanes in 1966. "[But] if you put people into a beautiful hall and don't give them quality, in two years you'll have an empty monument." Hanes, president of the Hanes Dye and Finishing Company, of Winston-Salem, North Carolina, confessed that the only thing "I don't know anything about, really, is opera," but added morosely to a reporter that it was quite a task to get customers for art in his home state. "I've learned more trying to sell tickets than from anything else. I can't think of anything harder, can you?"

Throughout the country it was agreed that potential customers had more and better opportunities to hear music than ever before. What was beginning to dawn was that there were not enough audiences to go around. The musical public, according to the Twentieth Century Fund report, was only five million in the United States, or about 4 percent of the population eighteen years of age or older. Blue-collar workers still barely made up 10 percent of audiences at performances.

During the "cultural boom," as before, the high-income group that made up the traditional audience was all that would attend presentations. Happily, other reasons for promoting new construction were found. It was good for business in general and gave communities a good name.

Another rationale was that though cultural centers had their faults, they were at least a beginning. But there was mounting evidence that arts centers could do more harm than good as cultural institutions. They could, for example, debase the potential level they were supposed to raise. The old saw that a bad job is better than no job turned out wrong. A bad job was never presented as a bad job. It was presented as a good job, and that is what happened in arts centers throughout the country. In some communities local social leaders played with arts centers while ignorant of the most elementary knowledge of either art or the operation of cultural institutions. This made for the worst distortions possible.

The jumbling of values seemed to rise from two sources: a reluctance to formulate any values and an absence of leaders who could do the formulating. From an economic standpoint, the results were often ludicrous. Businessmen promised that inherently money-losing institutions would henceforth not be run by strict box-office principles; then they interfered in choices of artists and repertory to insure maximum income at the box office.

And because essentially public activities were often governed by whim, there was a haphazard character to the cultural explosion. How else to explain mammoth cultural centers built to house small audiences? Or conversely, the curious notion that every performer deserves audiences for his talents, regardless of their worth.

Nearly 150 years ago, Alexis de Tocqueville, a French nobleman with liberal ideas, compared the outlooks of aristocratic and democratic nations in his masterful *Democracy in America*. "In aristocratic communities the people readily give themselves up to bursts of tumultuous and boisterous gaiety," the seer wrote. But in democracies the people preferred "the more serious and silent amusements which are like business and which do not drive business wholly out of their minds. An American . . . shuts himself up at home to drink. He thus enjoys two pleasures; he can go on thinking of his business and can get drunk decently by his own fireside."

De Tocqueville doubted that an aggressive, determined, ambitious, pragmatic, businesslike people such as the Americans would be capable of great artistic endeavors, despite their profound interest in community affairs. "In the United States," he reflected, "a wealthy man thinks that he owes it to public opinion to devote his leisure to some kind of industrial or commercial pursuit or to public business. He would think himself in bad repute if he employed his life solely in living."

# Epilogue: The Performing Arts
# in a Great Society

*"This report on the state of the performing arts in the United States is intended as a challenge, not an answer.*

*"Its purpose is to present a thoughtful assessment of the place of the performing arts in our national life and to identify the impediments to their greater welfare and to their wider enjoyment. Because the aim of this report is to suggest, to guide, to help point the way, its conclusions can be neither definitive nor final."*

—The Performing Arts: Problems and Prospects, *1965*

ONE FEATURE OF Kennedy's New Frontier carried forward into Johnson's Great Society was the way scholars, business leaders, foundation executives and others organized to probe, study, investigate, consider and ponder the nation's cultural problems. Discussion about the "cultural explosion" rose to an all-time high. Committees were called into existence to assess the organizations and institutions of the arts, to exhort the citizenry to greater efforts in behalf of culture.

A choice example was a thirty-member Rockefeller Brothers Fund panel composed primarily of leading businessmen but also including museum directors, theater producers, educators, administrators and custodians of the arts. Convened in 1963, it labored eighteen months to bring forth a report. In the best panel style, forty witnesses expert in the arts as well as government, education, management and labor were heard, four hundred persons were interviewed by the staff "individually or in small groups," one hundred corporations were surveyed by questionnaire, seventy-five officials of philanthropic institutions and performing-arts organizations presented their thoughts and eight states and forty-seven municipalities were surveyed to determine their support of the arts.

On the economic status of performing artists, the panel admitted encountering "considerable difficulties" in simply obtaining information. On the economic value of the arts, findings were evidently easier to come by. "Availability [of the arts] certainly encourages new firms to locate in a city and helps attract tourists and conventions" it says on page 81 of the report. But the weight of this finding is somewhat lessened by news on page 82 that "the typical American corporation has so far shown very little enthusiasm for financial support of the performing arts. Indeed, its contribution to philanthropy of all sorts is surprisingly small."

Overall, the panel was not discouraged by the disorganization and poverty it found in professional artistic organizations. "The potential for successful development of the performing arts is tremendous," it said—largely because millions of Americans have never yet attended a live professional performance. There are "untold numbers" who might become artists. There are "material resources" (meaning money) available if the nation just chooses to look for them.

Much space was devoted to these "material resources," but the basic finding was that neither foundations nor individuals nor the government nor business corporations were exactly champing at the bit to carry their share of the financial load. And if the general public put such a low priority on attendance at performances, one outcome predicted was an increasingly larger deficit in the budgets of even the most famous artistic institutions.

In advance of its investigation, the panel admitted to prejudices: "that the arts are not for a privileged few but for the many, that their place is not at the periphery of society but at its center, that they are not just a form of recreation but are of central importance to our well-being and happiness." It called for "high-quality, non-profit, professional organizations" in its conclusions:

Fifty permanent theater companies;

Fifty symphony orchestras whose members would also make up smaller musical groups;

Six regional opera groups, in addition to the four major resident companies we now have;

Six regional choral groups;

Six regional dance groups.

Fertile with suggestions, panelists recommended that physical plants be improved and expanded, territories of existing units revised, salary scales rationalized and efficiency improved by cutting down on standby time. In addition, the public had to be educated and a national information center set up to collect data and to facilitate communication between groups.

Given these stimuli, art in America would flourish.

Americans like committees that do thorough investigative jobs, and Rockefeller, the panel, the staff, witnesses and survey respondents were all justly praised for perspicacity and acumen. The blessings of distinguished men, undoubtedly in favor of more and better art to begin with, were obtained. An appearance of people hard at work on a problem was made.

On the other hand, little change occurred in the hearts and minds of the American public or its business leaders as a result of the report. Three years later National Industrial Conference Board figures still put corporate giving to the arts as only 2.8 percent of total corporate contributions. In some corporations, public relations men got busy. A life-insurance company bearing the name of a Revolutionary War patriot commissioned a series of oil paintings of its hero. This was announced a major gift to culture. A Business Committee for the Arts was formed in New York to help effect changes in the corporate pocketbook policy. But very few companies took inspiration from the examples of Texaco and the Joseph P. Schlitz Brewing Company in actually giving support to musical organizations.

If the panel's own conclusions are to be accepted, the basic problem to be faced during the next decade is not simply money. Nor is it construction, efficiency or education. It is whether the private sector is capable of producing leaders who will really lead. "The examples of virtually all the other great nations cannot be ignored," cautions the panel. "We have reached a point in our history when we must come to grips with the question of the role of government in our cultural life."

Nothing better exemplifies the lack of overall direction and stability than Lincoln Center in January 1969, the time of this writing. After seven years of operation, the center is in such grave difficulties that a drastic financial and management reorganization is underway. William Schuman has resigned as president and the administrative staff has been cut by a third. The entire programming department has been dropped, and support for some activities, such as the film festival, has been terminated.

Amyas Ames, chairman of Lincoln Center's executive committee, has explained that urban, racial and educational problems have crowded thoughts of the arts from the minds of prospective contributors. Sufficient funds are not being found to carry center activities; meanwhile, operating costs, especially overhead, are going up. Ames, who is also president of the New York Philharmonic's board of directors, points out that the orchestra's deficit is now $800,000 a year, partly because of its commitment to give players fifty-two weeks of employment annually. "The flow of blood must be stanched this year [via economies]," Ames warns. "Otherwise the running of Lincoln Center will have to be turned over to its constituents."

Beyond considerations of administrative effectiveness, Ames seems to be implying that the idea of a cultural center as a joint undertaking by major performing groups might just not be feasible. The proof finally, publicly and conclusively will be fiscal success. Yet it is precisely in fund raising that Lincoln Center has been most successful—thanks largely to volunteers such as Mr. Ames. Raising $178 million (by 1969) has proved that it is possible to find support for the arts. The techniques are now known and available to anyone who cares to study and to use them.

The problem is still money, all right, but before that it is attitude and approach. Throughout its history, Lincoln Center has had noble aims but has used some pretty uninspired operating principles to achieve them. The dream has been at war with the reality; lofty purposes have been diluted so that the center sometimes appears little more than a showcase for middlebrow tastes.

Take architecture, for example. At the center, group decisions via building committees are the rule, the belief prevailing that problems of design and function are too important to be left to professionals. With a few exceptions, results have been neither good nor bad. At best, buildings are "monumental" and functional like motels; at worst, there is no strong, single, unifying element to the whole center. Each constituent seems to have marched off on its own.

Take also the heavy reliance on "reputation." In the selection of architects, administrators, directors and other personnel the question posed was not, evidently, "Do I like his work and his style?" It was "Who knows him and what do they think of him?" "What has he produced, for whom and for how much?"

Robert Hoguet, a distinguished broker, once said that he knew nothing about physics but if he were appointed chairman of the Atomic Energy Committee and asked to appoint five top physicists, he could do the job. Hoguet would sit by the phone and "within four or five hours . . . would have the names of the 15 leading candidates for the posts and would know which ones were available."

Applying the same technique to the repertory theater, Hoguet diligently learned as much as he could about theatrical people. But this information could not forestall a series of misunderstandings he had with producers and directors, stretching from Whitehead and Kazan to Irving and Blau. These men are craftsmen in their fields as is Hoguet in his. The conclusion must be that there were no compatible objectives. The criterion of reputation alone did not offer enough information for meaningful choices. An observation Gay Talese once made about writers comes to mind: "One must be seen to exist, for now there is no other proof. There is no longer an identity in craft, only in self-promotion. There are no acts, only scenes."

Because the arts mirror society, and because society needs the definition and explanation that only the arts can provide, ways will be found to support them. Lincoln Center will survive, and so, probably, will most of the arts centers put up during the "cultural boom" of the 1950s. But whether the best procedure in the future is to trust to laissez-faire "do-it-yourself" tactics or to develop a sensible national policy is now a basic question. In the 1960s, as in the 1850s, music is still regarded vaguely as a Good Thing, and there is still honest confusion whether it is a Good Thing as a business, as a popular entertainment like a circus or as an affectation of the rich. If the Rockefeller Brothers panel report and Lincoln Center have done nothing else, they offer evidence that rich America can ignore the problems of the arts only at the risk of allowing famous artistic institutions to deteriorate.

Commitment. Perhaps that's one factor the panel forgot to consider. When more Henry Higginsons and Morton Baums decide what they like and take leadership, the arts in America are going to be well nourished, whether with corporate, with foundation or with government funds.

# Bibliography

## GENERAL REFERENCE WORKS

*Baker's Biographical Dictionary of Musicians*, revised by Nicolas Slonimsky. New York, 1958.
*Columbia Encyclopedia*, second edition. New York, 1950.
*Dictionary of American Biography*. New York, 1929.
*Die Musik in Geschichte und Gegenwart*. Kassel und Basel, 1949.
*Encyclopedia Americana*. New York and Chicago, 1965.
*Encyclopaedia Britannica*, 14th edition. New York and Chicago, 1967.
*Encyclopedia of American Facts and Dates*. New York, 1959.
*Grove's Dictionary of Music and Musicians*, third edition. New York, 1928.
*Grove's Dictionary of Music and Musicians*, fifth edition. New York, 1954.
Mattfeld, Julius, *Variety Music Cavalcade*. New York, 1952.
Morris, Richard B., editor, *Encyclopedia of American History*. New York, 1952.
Odell, George Clinton Densmore, *Annals of the New York Stage*. New York, 1931.
Scholes, Percy A., *The Oxford Companion to Music*, ninth edition. London, 1967.
Thompson, Oscar, editor, *The International Cyclopedia of Music and Musicians*, revised by Nicolas Slonimsky. New York, 1958.

## PERIODICALS

*Current Biography*. New York, 1940 ff.
*Dwight's Journal of Music*. Boston, 1852 ff.
*Musical America*. New York, 1898 ff.
*Musical Courier*. New York, 1880 ff.
*Musical Quarterly*. New York, 1915 ff.
*Musical Review and Choral Advocate*. New York, 1854–1855.
*Musical World and Times*. New York, 1852–1854.
*New York Herald Tribune*. New York, 1924 ff.

*New York Morning Herald*. New York, 1850–1924.
*New York Times*. New York, 1851 ff.
*New York Tribune*. New York, 1841–1924.


ARTICLES

Boretz, Benjamin, "Lincoln Center: Tomb of the Future." *The Nation* (March 22, 1965).
"Brightness in the Air." *Time* (December 18, 1964).
Cater, Douglass, "The Kennedy Look in the Arts." *Horizon* (September 1961).
Elliott, George P., "A Center in Search of a Role." *New York Times Magazine* (September 11, 1966).
Evett, Robert, "Passing Out Money Among Artists." *New Republic* (January 18, 1964).
Gelb, Arthur and Barbara, "Culture Makes a Hit at the White House." *New York Times Magazine* (January 28, 1962).
Goldin, Milton, "Commerce, Concerts and Critics." *Music Educators Journal* (April 1960).
———, "Music Travels Westward." *Arts and Science* (Spring 1967).
———, "New York's First Lincoln Center." *Musical Courier* (September 1961).
———, "The Great Rubinstein Road Show." *High Fidelity* (September 1966).
———, "The Napoleon of Impresarios." *Music Journal* (June 1966).
———, "The Musical Stock Market." *Amor Artis Bulletin* (October 1965).
———, "The Food of Love, the Lot of the Caterer." *Amor Artis Bulletin* (February 1967).
———, "The Lyric Temple of the South." *Amor Artis Bulletin* (April 1968).
Gover, Robert, "'Culture' Comes to Indianapolis." *New York Times Magazine* (December 24, 1967).
Grunfeld, Fred, "What's the Score?" *Reporter* (October 15, 1959).
Hanks, Nancy, "Shall We Ration the Arts?" *Bulletin of the Foundation Library Center* (March 1968).
Hannon, Leslie, "American Culture?" *New York Times Magazine* (February 16, 1964).

Heckscher, August, "Ordering a Cultural Explosion." *Horizon* (December 1962).

———, "The Central Role of the Arts." *Music Journal* (January 1964).

———, "The Danger of Amateurism in the Arts." *International Musician* (June 1963).

Hentoff, Nat, "Lost Soloists Along the Concert Trail." *Reporter* (April 1958).

"High Cs in Big D." *Time* (December 2, 1966).

"Inside Job." *Newsweek* (December 21, 1964).

Johnson, H. Earle, "Some 'First Performances' in America." *Journal of the American Musicological Society* (Fall 1952).

———, "The Germania Musical Society." *Musical Quarterly* (January 1953).

"Kahn, Morgan, and 'Salome.'" *Saturday Review* (May 30, 1964).

[Kennedy, John], "The Late President's Last Reflections on the Arts." *Saturday Review* (March 28, 1964).

Kupferberg, Herbert, "The Culture Monopoly at Lincoln Center." *Harper's Magazine* (October 1961).

———, "The Mess at Lincoln Center." *New York Herald Tribune* (December 27, 1964).

Lazare, Christopher, "Da Ponte, the Bearer of Culture." *The New Yorker* (March 25, 1944).

Lowry, W. McNeil, "The Foundation and the Arts." *Music Journal* (March 1964).

Lynes, Russell, "Who Wants Art?" *Harper's Magazine* (July 1965).

Mannes, Marya, "They're Cultural, but Are They Cultured?" *New York Times Magazine* (July 9, 1961).

Martin, John, "The Ford Foundation's Ballet Grants." *Saturday Review* (March 28, 1964).

Mayer, Martin, "Ford Moves In on the Arts." *Horizon* (January 1962).

Moses, Robert, "Needed: New Medicis for New Art Centers." *New York Times Magazine* (May 10, 1959).

Mueller, John H., "The Social Nature of Musical Taste." *Journal of Research in Music Education* (Fall 1956).

Rich, Alan, "Cultural Centers Without Culture?" *New York Herald Tribune* (January 3, 1965).

———, "This Way to the Abattoir." *Allegro* (November 1963).

Rockefeller 3rd, John D., "The Evolution: Birth of a Great Center." *New York Times Magazine* (September 23, 1965).

Rogers, Francis, "America's First Grand Opera Season." *The Musical Quarterly* (January 1915).

Saerchinger, César, "Musical Landmarks in New York." *Musical Quarterly* (January, October 1920).

Sargeant, Winthrop, "Requiem for a Lightweight." *New Yorker* (January 5, 1963).

Schonberg, Harold C., "Man to Orchestrate Lincoln Center." *New York Times Magazine* (December 31, 1961).

———, "The National 'Cultural Explosion' Is Phony," *Saturday Evening Post* (July 13, 1963).

———, "Presenting S. Hurok, Impresario." *New York Times Magazine* (April 26, 1959).

———, "The Lincoln Center Vision Takes Form." *New York Times Magazine* (December 11, 1960).

Schuman, William, "Have We 'Culture'? Yes—and No." *New York Times Magazine* (September 22, 1963).

Sklare, Marshall, "The Trouble with 'Our Crowd.'" *Commentary* (January 1968).

Stoddard, Hope, "America Builds for Music." *International Musician* (March 1965).

Straight, Michael, "Something for the Arts: Cultural Life in a Great Society." *New Republic* (March 13, 1965).

Terry, Walter, "Ford Blows Up a Storm." *New York Herald Tribune* (January 12, 1964).

Toffler, Alvin, "Detroit Culture: Bumper to Bumper." *Show* (June 1962).

Udall, Stewart L., "The Arts as a National Resource." *Saturday Review* (March 28, 1964).

Young, Warren R., "The Remarkable Ford Foundation." *Life* (September 21, 1962).

## BOOKS

Aldrich, Richard, *Concert Life in New York 1902–1923*. New York, 1941.

———, *Musical Discourses*. New York, 1928.

Amory, Cleveland, *Who Killed Society?* New York, 1960.

Asbury, Herbert, *The French Quarter*. New York, 1936.

Barnum, P. T., *Barnum's Own Story* [1855, 1869–1888]. New York, 1961.

Barzun, Jacques, *Music in American Life*. New York, 1956.

Baumol, William J., and Bowen, William G., *Performing Arts: the Economic Dilemma*. New York, 1966.

Benét, Laura, *Enchanting Jenny Lind*. New York, 1939.

Berlioz, Hector, *Evenings with the Orchestra* [1852], translated from the French by Jacques Barzun. New York, 1956.

Birmingham, Stephen, *Our Crowd*. New York, 1967.

Bispham, David, *A Quaker Singer's Recollections*. New York, 1920.

Bowen, Catherine Drinker, *Free Artist: the Story of Anton and Nicholas Rubinstein*. New York, 1939.

Bradley, Van Allen, *Music for the Millions: the Kimball Piano and Organ Story*. Chicago, 1957.

Burt, Nathaniel, *The Perennial Philadelphians*. Boston, 1963.

Butterfield, Roger, *The American Past*. Second edition. New York, 1966.

Carnegie, Andrew, *The Autobiography of Andrew Carnegie*. Boston, 1920.

Carse, Adam, *The Life of Jullien*. Cambridge, England, 1951.

———, *The Orchestra from Beethoven to Berlioz*. Cambridge, England, 1948.

Chase, Gilbert, *America's Music from the Pilgrims to the Present*. New York, 1955.

Chasins, Abram, *Speaking of Pianists*. New York, 1961.

Coad, Oral Sumner, and Mims, Edwin, Jr., *The American Stage*. New Haven, 1929.

Cone, John F., *Oscar Hammerstein's Manhattan Opera Company*. Norman, Okla., 1964.

Da Ponte, Lorenzo, *Memoirs of Lorenzo Da Ponte*, translated by Elizabeth Abbott. New York, 1959.

Damrosch, Walter, *My Musical Life*. New York, 1924.

Davison, James William, *From Mendelssohn to Wagner*. London, 1912.

Demuth, Norman, *An Anthology of Musical Criticism*. London, 1947.

Dickens, Charles, *American Notes for General Circulation* [1842]. New York, 1961.

Eames, Emma, *Some Memories and Reflections*. New York, 1927.

Eaton, Quaintance, editor, *Musical U.S.A.* New York, 1949.

———, *Opera Caravan*. New York, 1957.

Ellis, Edward R., *The Epic of New York*. New York, 1966.

Elson, Louis C., *The History of American Music*. New York, 1925.

Erskine, John, *My Life in Music*. New York, 1950.

Ewen, David, *Music Comes to America.* New York, 1942.
Farwell, Arthur, and Darby, W. Dermot, *Music in America.* New York, 1932.
Finck, Henry, *My Adventures in the Golden Age of Music.* New York, 1926.
————, *Paderewski and His Art.* New York, 1895.
Ferrier, Winifred, *Kathleen Ferrier.* London, 1959.
Flesch, Carl, *The Memoirs of Carl Flesch,* translated from the German by Hans Keller. New York, 1958.
Franko, Sam, *Chords and Discords.* New York, 1938.
Galbraith, John Kenneth, *The Affluent Society.* New York, 1958.
Garden, Mary, and Biancolli, Louis, *Mary Garden's Story.* New York, 1951.
Gatti-Casazza, Giulio, *Memories of the Opera.* New York, 1941.
Gerson, R. A., *Music in Philadelphia.* Philadelphia, 1940.
Gipson, Richard McCandless, *The Life of Emma Thursby 1845–1931.* New York, 1940.
Gottschalk, Louis Moreau, *Notes of a Pianist.* Philadelphia, 1881.
Grigoriev, S. L., *The Diaghilev Ballet 1909–1929.* Baltimore, 1960.
Grout, Donald Jay, *A Short History of Opera.* New York, 1947.
*Hans von Bülow, a Biographical Sketch, His Visit to America.* Boston, 1875.
Harrison, Harry P., and Detzer, Karl, *Culture Under Canvas.* New York, 1958.
Hauser, Arnold, *The Social History of Art.* New York, 1958.
Hecht, Ben, *A Child of the Century.* New York, 1954.
Heylbut, Rose, and Gerber, Amé, *Backstage at the Opera.* New York, 1937.
Holbrook, Stewart H., *The Age of the Moguls.* New York, 1953.
Hone, Philip, *The Diary of Philip Hone* [1828–1851]. New York, 1927.
Howard, J. T., *Our American Music.* New York, 1939.
Howe, M. A. DeWolfe, *The Boston Symphony Orchestra 1881–1931.* Boston, 1931.
Hurok, S., *Impresario.* New York, 1946.
————, *S. Hurok Presents: A Memoir of the Dance World.* New York, 1953.
Huxtable, Ada Louise, *Classic New York.* Garden City, 1964.
Johnson, H. Earle, *Symphony Hall, Boston.* Boston, 1950.
Kane, Harnett T., *Queen New Orleans: City by the River.* New York, 1949.
Keefer, Lubov, *Baltimore's Music: The Haven of the American Composer.* Baltimore, 1963.

Klein, Herman, *Musicians and Mummers*. London, 1925.

———, *Unmusical New York*. London, 1910.

Kolodin, Irving, *The Story of the Metropolitan Opera 1883–1950*. New York, 1953.

Kraus, Michael and Vera, *Family Album for Americans*. New York, 1961.

Krehbiel, Henry Edward, *Chapters of Opera*. New York, 1909.

———, *More Chapters of Opera*. New York, 1910.

Lahee, Henry Charles, *Annals of Music in America*. Boston, 1922.

———, *Famous Pianists of To-day and Yesterday*. Boston, 1900.

———, *Famous Violinists of To-day and Yesterday*. Boston, 1902.

Lang, Paul Henry, editor, *One Hundred Years of Music in America*. New York, 1961.

Leiser, Clara, *Jean de Reszke and the Great Days of Opera*. New York, 1934.

Lengyel, Cornel, editor, *History of Music in San Francisco*. San Francisco, 1939–1942.

Lochner, Louis P., *Fritz Kreisler*. New York, 1950.

Loesser, Arthur, *Men, Women and Pianos: A Social History*. New York, 1954.

Longley, Marjorie, et al., *America's Taste: 1851–1959*. New York, 1960.

MacClintock, Lander, *Orpheus in America: Offenbach's Diary of His Journey to the New World*. Bloomington, Indiana, 1957.

Macdonald, Dwight, *The Ford Foundation*. New York, 1956.

McDonald, Forrest, *Insull*. Chicago, 1962.

Mapleson, James Henry, *The Mapleson Memoirs 1848–1888*. London, 1888.

Marek, George, editor, *The World Treasury of Grand Opera*. New York, 1957.

Maretzek, Max, *Crotchets and Quavers*. New York, 1855.

———, *Sharps and Flats*. New York, 1890.

Marks, Edward B., *They All Had Glamour*. New York, 1944.

Marryat, Frederick, *A Diary in America* [1839]. New York, 1962.

Mattfeld, Julius, *A Hundred Years of Grand Opera in New York 1825–1925*. New York, 1926.

Matz, Mary Jane, *The Many Lives of Otto Kahn*. New York, 1963.

Miers, Earl Schenck, editor, *The American Story*. London, 1957.

Morris, Lloyd, *Curtain Time*. New York, 1953.

———, *Incredible New York*. New York, 1951.

Mueller, John Henry, *The American Symphony Orchestra.* Bloomington, Indiana, 1951.

Myers, Gustavus, *History of the Great American Fortunes.* New York, 1936.

Nevins, Allan, and Thomas, Milton Halsey, editors, *The Diary of George Templeton Strong.* New York, 1952.

Newman, Ernest, *Wagner as Man and Artist.* New York, 1924.

Noble, Helen, *Life with the Met.* New York, 1954.

Paderewski, Ignace Jan, and Lawton, Mary, *The Paderewski Memoirs.* New York, 1938.

Peltz, Mary Ellis, *Behind the Gold Curtain: The Story of the Metropolitan Opera 1883–1950.* New York, 1950.

*The Performing Arts: Problems and Prospects.* New York, 1965.

Pougin, Arthur, *Marietta Alboni.* Paris, 1912.

Ritter, Frédéric Louis, *Music in America.* New York, 1883.

Robinson, Francis, *Caruso: His Life in Pictures.* New York, 1957.

Rolland, Romain, *Essays in Music.* New York, 1948.

Rowsome, Frank, Jr., *They Laughed When I Sat Down.* New York, 1959.

Ryan, Thomas, *Recollections of an Old Musician.* New York, 1899.

Samaroff, Olga, *An American Musician's Story.* New York, 1939.

Schickel, Richard, *The World of Carnegie Hall.* New York, 1960.

Schonberg, Harold C., *The Great Pianists.* New York, 1963.

Sheean, Vincent, *Oscar Hammerstein, I: The Life and Exploits of an Impresario.* New York, 1956.

Shultz, Gladys Denny, *Jenny Lind: The Swedish Nightingale.* New York, 1962.

Smith, Cecil, *Musical Comedy in America.* New York, 1950.

———, *Worlds of Music.* New York, 1952.

Smith, Mortimer, *The Life of Ole Bull.* Princeton, 1943.

*Souvenir Programs of Great Moments of Music at Carnegie Hall.* New York, 1959.

Spaeth, Sigmund, *Fifty Years with Music.* New York, 1959.

Steinway, Theodore E., *People and Pianos: A Century of Service to Music.* New York, 1953.

Still, Bayrd, *Mirror for Gotham.* New York, 1956.

Strakosch, Maurice, *Souvenirs d'un Impresario.* Paris, 1887.

Swan, Howard, *Music in the Southwest.* San Marino, Calif., 1952.

Swanberg, W. A., *Jim Fisk: The Career of an Improbable Rascal.* London, 1960.

Tallant, Robert, *The Romantic New Orleanians.* New York, 1950.

Tatum, George, *Penn's Great Town*. Philadelphia, 1961.

Taubman, Howard, *The Making of the American Stage*. New York, 1965.

Timberlake, Craig, *The Bishop of Broadway: The Life and Work of David Belasco*. New York, 1954.

Tocqueville, Alexis de, *Democracy in America* [1835]. New York, 1954.

Toffler, Alvin, *The Culture Consumers: Art and Influence in America*. New York, 1965.

Upton, George P., *Theodore Thomas: a Musical Autobiography*. Chicago, 1905.

Upton, William T., *William Henry Fry*. New York, 1954.

Valentine, Alan, *1913: America Between Two Worlds*. New York, 1962.

Wallace, Irving, *The Fabulous Showman: The Life and Times of P. T. Barnum*. New York, 1959.

Werner, M. R., *It Happened in New York*. New York, 1957.

Westrup, J. A., *An Introduction to Musical History*. London, 1955.

Williams, J. W., *The Lusty Texans of Dallas*. New York, 1960.

# Index